Baguettes and Blanquette

Edited by Jo O'Neill

ISBN: 978-1-3999-8409-6

Herstories from the Aude Valley

HAT
FACTORY
BOOKS

CONTENTS

Life is either a daring adventure or nothing at all.
Helen Keller

Foreword

October 2020. Lunch.

I'm with a bunch of women I hardly know, in a restaurant in the South of France, celebrating a birthday. Listening to everyone's chatter, I realise that we have one fundamental thing in common. We have all made the momentous decision to leave our countries of birth to come and live in this little town in the Aude Valley. We all have a story to tell that has led to our emigration, drawn us to here.

In response to the question *Why here?*, I had often heard phrases such as *It has a kind of magic that just draws you here* or *I didn't find this place, this place found me*. So I wanted to explore this idea further and find out exactly how and why a group of women from all over the world chose to be in the same location.

And so, an idea began to grow in my head. We were coming into the second winter lockdown of the Covid pandemic. We would need to fill our time, to find productive, memorable things to do. Why not write? Why not tell our stories? Our journeys.

There is a little market town, nestled in the foothills of the French Pyrenees. Here are the true stories of our ten lives, our journeys to this beautiful place.

Jo O'Neill

Minna's Story

A Mostly French Story

It is August 2023. La Place de la République is rammed, the bars are overflowing. The band on the stage reverberates high decibel rock off three sides of the square into the fourth void over the river, and up up to bounce back from the overhanging walls of the ruined blue-lit Chateau. Faces red from dancing negotiate their way through the all-age crowd, past the masked creepy-clowns, back to a space at a table and their drink and their friends, or to lean against the railings to catch their breath. In the heat of the summer it is party time. For the best part of a month, music of all genres, DJs, dancers, and troupes performing what are billed as native rituals appear nightly before a grateful, tolerant and occasionally bemused population. At this time of year the influx of second- home owners swell the crowd. Holiday makers fill the Air B&Bs, and the hotels, and the rented rooms of the town. Shutters long closed creak open, houses have eyes again. Chattering-bird suitcases are wheeled along uneven pavements by strangers who struggle with unfamiliar key codes and temperamental keys. The newcomers walk around in flocks, taking photographs, looking up and around, talking loudly amongst themselves in their native tongues. They come from all over, from the EU and beyond, from America, from the East, from the sad self-exiled UK where the theft of freedom of movement hits hardest. The little town calls them, and they return year after year. Some never leave. Some arrive and surprise themselves by asking without knowing why, 'Why would I leave and go anywhere else?' And they stay and grow roots in this old old settlement place beside the River Aude that gives the place its energy and its flow. The waters sometimes rush urgently, noisily through rock and gorge, or flow slowly, spreading calmly and widely from bank to bank, the clean brown fisherman-pleasing shallows casting a zen-like spell. The river gave the town its industry. From the seventeenth century to the nineteenth the muscular radeliers crewed rafts of trees downstream. Then the hat making came, that used the strength of the water to power the terrifying machinery, to wash the bleach from the wool, to rinse the dyes, to thrust the moulds onto the damp felt to shape every kind of hat from Napoleonic tricorne to trilby, from beret to cloche to wide- brimmed Hollywood Glamour. The craft of wool felting used in hat manufacture in the area was, so legend has it, brought back from Silesia, an area in south-western Poland, by soldiers in the Imperial Army assigned to nearby Bucharach. Hundreds of thousands of hats were produced every year for nigh on a century or more, in this little valley in the south of France. Just one recently reopened factory, at Montazels near Esperaza, employs and trains a few people to make hats using the old machinery in the old ways, and also hosts musical events. The same building was used to imprison over nine hundred Spanish Republican refugees from Franco's conquest of Catalonia in January 1939, in terrible conditions, starving and disease-ridden, with only six toilets between them all. Life is contrast. On the dual carriageway north of the town, with its familiar multicoloured logo, is the Formica factory opened in 1952 when the American founders expanded the company into Europe. It closed in 2003, and is now a centre of excellence, making structured press plates for Formica plants worldwide. For the fiftieth anniversary of the moon landing they created a laminate design to represent the surface of the moon, available in nine dramatic shades.

***

It is June 1970. The white cliffs pull into perspective behind the churning wake of the ferry from Newhaven. She is eighteen and this is the first time she has left the shores that she has never really felt native within, just trapped upon. Two girls are going to hitchhike to Italy. She has a tangible lump in her throat as she raises her hand and waves, but at what she is not certain. They reach Dieppe, find the road to Paris, and put out their thumbs. She feels at home the minute she steps onto this other shore, onto The Continent, a mere twenty-five miles away from what already feels like a previous life. Or maybe she is stepping back into a previous life, who knows, but the smell of it is different and oh so familiar. France. Even now, whenever she drinks sterilised milk in a cool mouthful, she is straightaway back on the road, hitchhiking to Paris, to Florence and Rome, to Munich and Amsterdam. France, Italy, Austria, Germany, Holland. That six week trip, by auto stop, shapes her dream of living in Europe. They hitchhike to Paris, down to Marseilles, along the Côte d'Azur through San Tropez, the seafront cafés and restaurants then affordable, to Cannes, to Nice, en route to Italy. The only bum ride with a middle-aged man, his hand moving in rhythm under the towel on his lap as he drives. Annoyed by their mocking protests he dumps them on the mountain road above Monaco. At the passport check at Ventimiglia near Menton, the admiration for the two girls is made evident without threat. Linguistically a kind of Eurosprakel oils the wheels of communication and gets them where they need to go. In Florence she spends her days sketching in the Uffizi gallery, sitting on the floor, and goes to have another look at Michelangelo's David whenever she wants to. This is before the days of timed slots booked three months in advance. In the Piazza della Signoria, as she sits at the foot of the replica David, two American women pause and look up, *Gee*, says one to the other, *They've got one just like we have in Noo York*. She counts her blessings. They sleep, among other places, under an evergreen bush near the Colosseum in Rome, awoken and challenged by a gardener in the morning, who upon comprehending that they were English, merely points his finger at his temple to indicate their insanity and goes away. They stay there two or three nights, exploring Rome, warm and cosy, leaving their possessions on the dried leaves mattressing the ground in the space under the living tent.

It is 1971. In the summer break from drama school in London she travels with three others in an ancient overheating radiator-cap-blowing Landrover via Germany, through a then united Yugoslavia, around a closed Albania, and on to the southernmost part of the Peloponnese in Greece, to Githion, then a tiny village with a one-pole fixed tap on the beach for a shower. Here she basks in the mystic benevolent optimism of a Supreme Being whilst under the influence of psychedelics, indeed a different kind of journey.

Dear reader, it was the seventies. On the way back they camp near Athens, and late one night in the city, they ignore a single wire fence and scramble up a scrubby hillside to find themselves on the Acropolis, a moonlit silent soul-turning miracle. She returns to Athens three decades later with her son, and their first sight, from the hotel window, of the floodlit Acropolis, gifts them the same shafts of awe and wonder.

It is Easter 1972, she and a friend hitchhike up the Loire Valley, arriving at Amboise for the annual wine festival. A two franc fee permits multiple entries to a long line of wine-makers all keen to offer samples of their products. On their third trip down the long sloping floor of the cellars she receives a proposal of marriage from a vendor impressed solely by her ability to remain upright. The white wines taste of honey and the red wines taste of berries and wood, and they picnic with both on the banks of the Loire, accompanied by baguette and tinned mackerel. She can't keep away from France. It beckons constantly.

It is 1974, in February, and she somehow gets herself to Perpignan to stay with her current crush, only to be met at the Gare by a blond Norwegian who informs her in stilted English that her intended beau has fled to a London hospital nursing a severely inflamed testicle. But he has left her the keys to his village house, and to a huge Jaguar car belonging to a Hollywood producer. It has two fuel tanks. She puts five-francs worth into alternate sides, is laughed at by gorgeous young petrol attendants, and zooms about the Pyrénées-Orientales for very short distances at a time. She finds out later she is totally uninsured. She invites several entirely French speaking new acquaintances to celebrate her twenty-second birthday, and could have stayed for ever. She has to leave to fulfil a contract for eight months at Pitlochry Festival Theatre in Scotland, where she lives in a near-derelict cottage on the edge of a feudal estate up the road in Moulin. The rent is one pound a week, and there is a circle of magic stones, thirteen outer and seven inner, a few steps away in the trees.

It's 1979, she goes to Hollywood, full of optimism, and stays with generous and tolerant friends in Topanga Canyon. She gets herself some meetings with well known producers, but is not picked up. She does however discover stand up comedy at The Comedy Store on Sunset Boulevard in Los Angeles. She sits nursing her one affordable margarita, and longs to be on stage with the others. It takes her twenty-seven years to manage it, that darned parrot on her shoulder all that time squawking *You didn't have the bottle, you didn't have the bottle.*

It is 1982, in a production of Danton's Death at the National Theatre the hiatus at the end of Act One is a powerful rendering of the Marseillaise, from all over the auditorium by the assembled sans- culottes of whom she is one. Previously assembled on stage cheering a blood-stained guillotine, this involves a very fast run from backstage to front of house. She finds herself in the Circle not only out of breath as the band strikes up, but also choked and tearful. This lump in her throat has never gone away, and she still stands gulping and silent whenever the opening to the French national anthem sounds. Now she lets those tears roll down her cheeks. Some umbilical magnet pulls her back and back again to France.

It is 1984. She travels to New Zealand to work on a film, and stops to acclimatise to the southern hemisphere in The Cook Islands, on Rarotonga, an exotic cultural shift. Living alone in a rented shack ten yards from the beach, at night she can hear the sound of the Pacific Ocean beyond the line of Maori graves, and the drumming of many drums. She is astonished by this Polynesian parallel universe, a world she never knew existed. She stays away from London for nine months in New Zealand and in Australia. She sees, and cannot believe, on June 18th, the appalling scenes of British police pitted against British miners at Orgreave, crackling onto a small black and white television screen in Wellington. Thatcher's destructive grip on Britain's societal structure was tightening. Tories, it seems, cannot resist tearing the fabric of the country apart, in whatever decade or century they hold the reins of power.

It is 1991. She rents a room in Paris for the month of August from Brad, a young American student in the throes of an affair with one of his mother's friends. It is in a mansion on Avenue Georges Mandel, but the grandiosely titled apartment is a tiny attic garret, a maid's room under the eaves. The double windows open onto a small lead covered space before the gutter begins from where there is a spectacular view of Le Tour Eiffel at a dreamlike nearness, illuminated from sundown until one o'clock in the morning. The other room, a kitchen cum shower looks out onto rooftops and chimney pots, and every morning she feeds dry baguette to the cooing pigeons who swoop in hordes. There is a Formica topped leaf-table, two fragile antique chairs, a TV watchable only with severe neck strain due to its perch on top of the wardrobe, and a permanent scuttling residency of light brown cockroaches. She keeps a firm-soled shoe within reach of the mattress on the floor that was the bed, and scrapes the squished and bloodied remains onto the balcony every morning. She sleeps alert to the touch of nuclear resistant roach feet traversing her face in the night. The telephone in the flat needs to be turned back on. Her young landlord has, without informing her, blocked phone calls outside Paris. She spends the first two days thinking that lines to London and the rest of France are permanently engaged, until she manages to decipher *We are unable to connect your call* from the recorded robot. *But there's a phone box on the street right outside the front door,* Brad had whined. *I cannot always stand in a phone box*, she had said, *what if I have to make a call in the middle of the night?* Brad had not shown the least remorse. Brad did not yet know about having to make phone calls in the middle of the night. One day she sees a possible future self on the platform as she waits at Étoile for the Pigalle connection. A version of how she might be in fifteen or twenty years time, hair scraped back, mixed with grey, glasses on a chain, a light blue Indian cotton suit, easily hand washed. Earnestly studying the Métro map, the woman was travelling with a youth of seventeen or so, perhaps a son produced late in life at forty-one or forty-two. Whether fantasy or a prediction this miracle indeed came to pass two years later, shared with a loved but temporary passing- through husband. How she had foreseen it she will never know.

In the 1980s it is either ferry or fly to France, but from 1994 The Eurostar, that wondrous metal worm emerging through an escape tunnel on to French soil, enables and encourages frequent trips to Paris. In the late nineties she takes her small single parented son, an enthusiastic fellow voyager whose first visit to the City of Love had been in utero. Now he walks miles, from the steps of Montmartre to the Rive Gauche. The Rue Mouffetard is in the 5th arrondissement, leading down from Place de la Contrescarpe, the home of Jean-Paul Sartre and Simone de Beauvoir. Ernest Hemingway lived just round the corner. This is the street where his mother's living-in-Paris fantasies are centred, as she gazes up through windows at beamed ceilings. He likes the patisseries and the restaurants. They ascend The Eiffel Tower right to the top, they sail a boat in the pond in Les Jardins des Tuileries. He rides a proud paint scuffed white horse on the carousel, he too seems very at home in France. Her spirit is willing but her courage fails her when contemplating a total physical move, rooted as she is by the familiarity of both career and family tentacles. Frequent cross- channelling happens by ferry, hovercraft, or whatever mode of transport is on special half-term offer. Nausicaá, the huge aquarium centre at Boulogne becomes a regular destination via a day return sailing to Calais, sometimes bearing cousins too. They go to Biarritz, they go to Normandy, they go to the Charente, they go to Paris again and again, they know how lucky they are to have friends in France. They go to Athens, they go to Venice, but those are other stories.

In 2020 when first she came to Carcassonne, she had forgotten about Perpignan, geography not being one of her strong points, and thought herself a stranger to the Aude. Many months later she remembered leaving Paris when that month in 1991 was up, and heading for Spain. By train. As they reached the south, *Montpellier* was announced by an unseen voice in five languages, French, English, Spanish, Italian and German. People got off, people got on, different people with different luggage. At Beziers the station clock had said ten past five as the train pulled slowly to a halt. Again people got off, people got on, different people with different suitcases. Beziers Cathedral rose high above the rest of the city, encased in scaffolding. Now a dust cloud is rising from an old truck driving through a vineyard. All vineyards now, vineyard after vineyard. At Narbonne, several people grab their bags to change for Toulouse, and two older ladies struggle to get their suitcase off the rack. A younger girl goes to their aid. The countryside grows ever more arid, with almost bare outcrops on rock-filled horizons. Churches and what look like monasteries appear, settle in vision, then vanish. The heavy green-grey that she had thought to be a storm-filled sky reveals itself to be an inlet of the Mediterranean Sea, shimmering in the sunlight. An entire small village on an island, fishing nets, fishing boats. The little bells ring again, *Mesdames et Messieurs, we are arriving at Perpignan*. So she has been here before, twice, five and three decades ago, and has now found her way back.

It is 1999. She supplements her income with a passion for portrait photography, and has a tiny gallery in Shepherds Bush. She hopes to entice the artistic clique down Holland Park Avenue from Notting Hill Gate, but they don't come, and after a year she sadly takes down the sign of the White Elephant at Gallery 44. She takes her small son to live in the wilds of Herefordshire so that he can get to know the names of trees, and his grandparents. He enjoys getting thoroughly muddy at Saturday football.

In 2002 they go back to Menton and pass through what had been the border check between France and Italy, and there is the same white building, abandoned now, squatting empty in the middle of the road. The relief of no borders, of being part of this European Union, for so many years so embracing, so freeing, so joyful, so normal. Until 2016, when the small minded, mean spirited, tax haven preserving, money conceived misbegotten birth of Brexit rendered Britain once more an outcast from the Mediterranean and beyond. Britain now dwindled into Little Britain. Like rats in a sack the bewildered population bickers, feeding on the scattered daily crusts and crumbs of dissent, scandal, and petty attacks, designed deliberately to distract and distort. 'Shock, Horror, My Neighbour Moved My Bin' makes headline news in the demeaned bought and paid for British media. Who pays the piper calls the tune. The country is visibly turning in on itself. She is not going to 'Not Talk about Brexit' because perhaps that is why she is here, now. To leave behind the flesh eating populist right-wing madness infecting the country. To avoid the unchallenged corruption of a political system that brooks no interference as it gleefully monetises every aspect of the public realm; a mindset so greedy, and so amoral, that a viral pandemic targeting the breathing apparatus of our species presents itself as an opportunity to profit from death. All and everything puts Money into the back pockets and offshore accounts of the charlatans and their friends, with ever less pretence of governance, as the government wrings the country dry. It may take an earthquake or starvation to shake the population out of their apathy. Has she run away? She is not sure. Until she finds her voice she is best occupied, she feels, by keeping her powder dry. By being somewhere where she does not on a daily basis wake shredded and incapacitated by rage at injustice, rendered helpless by the shapeshifting faceless implacable foe she can name only as Mammon. Whilst living in Andalucia for six months in her thirties someone asks her *Are you running away?* She replies as if it is a thought she'd never had before, *No, I think I'm running towards*. Always that certain feeling that the future is ahead, she predicts her last words will be *But no, not now, I've still got to . . .*

It is 2006, back in London she starts to do stand-up comedy and that parrot hops down from her shoulder, silenced at last. Fulfilling the ambition long-held since that first knot of excitement in her stomach in LA is Very Scary Indeed for the first three hundred or so gigs, then wonderfully freeing. She writes her own reviews for her first show, *Strange Muffled Sounds from the Audience* - My Weakly. *Mistress of her own Asylum* - A Bystander. She was invited to start a Comedy Club in a pub in King's Cross, which ran for a year or so until the owners of the pub ran off to Spain with what little profit they hadn't snorted up their noses, leaving their many creditors high and dry, or just dry. She gains a teaching qualification and that fills the ever-looming financial gaps. A solo comedy show coincides with the London Olympics; *Comedian goes for gold without the aid of visible knee supports. Share her vagaries of mind as she muses on Acronyms, MPs side hustles, Elusive pensions and why Time Goes Faster, as she eases arthritically into her Prime.* The flyer features her head superimposed onto a CGI generated lithe young lycra clad body on the starting line. Hilarious. She might do it again one day. With the benefit of hindsight her feminist humour might have been a tad oblique for mainstream tastes. But feedback from audiences of all ages over the years confirmed that she was doing stuff that resonated and made people laugh. No greater joy.

It's 2010. They are in Paris when they get the call that her father is in intensive care following a fall downstairs at midnight, as he was taking the morning tea tray upstairs. He died ten days later of pneumonia, brought on by fractured ribs and collarbone, in Hereford Hospital, with a harsh tube down his dear once beautiful tenor-voiced throat. That was a substantial bummer. She adored him. With her now widowed mother she had a relationship that could at best be described as fractious, as they vied for position and argued about politics. This continued on its trajectory for another decade until her mother succumbed to a massive stroke at the age of ninety-seven, at the very end of the first long Covid lockdown. Another bummer. She adored her mother too.

Victor Hugo also had his part to play on her journey. Her mother's grandmother, Joséphine, born in 1885, was the daughter of Aimable, one of several housekeepers to the legend during his sojourn on Guernsey. Of course she was going to be drawn to France, she had actual French blood coursing through her veins. She was one sixteenth French on the distaff side, and on her father's side descended from a Norman cousin of William the Conqueror, who fought alongside him in the successful invasion of England in 1066. Now that had been an invasion, like the Romans before them. Successive UK Home Secretaries perhaps need to study history, before tarring a few thousand soaking wet economic migrants with the same brush. There had been little chance of escaping her direction of travel, though she had not thought of it in terms of dna before. Not until one day when she crossed a particular Pont Vieux into a particular Place de la Republique with its shade of plane trees over restaurant tables, and felt so strongly that she could pause there. Over time she observes that people arrive here weighed down by baggage crammed with old lives, which all goes into some metaphorical left luggage depository on the edge of town. Pasts are stacked on shelves to be reclaimed by ticket as and when, or never. Packages gather dust, lose their labels and become untraceable, eventually being sold off as curios with unknown contents, at a local Vide Grenier in aid of the town's many stray cats.

***

It is 2023 and she drives, nay bowls, westwards down the near-empty white roads of the plain between the eastern end of the Pyrénées and the ever vigilant ruins of the impossibly positioned clifftop castles. The Chateaux of Peyrepertuse and of Quéribus, perched on seemingly inaccessible crags, still stand guard along the plain so much fought over by France and Spain, the whole area known as the Country of the Cathars. The beauty of this road through Maury, Saint Paul de Fenouillet and Caudiés never fails to astonish the traveller. She rounds a corner, full into the looming gaze of the Chateau of Puilarens, and tries to imagine the lives the occupants led there centuries before. There must have been a medieval version of deliveroo back then, or she hopes so. She turns north at the roundabout before Axat, and traverses the Gorges de la Pierre-Lys, through the tunnel hacked out by Abbé Félix Armand in 1781. Soon she comes to rest, like a homing pigeon, in a street bearing his name. This is a healing place, this town beside the waters of the Aude, on their journey from the lake high in the Pyrénées from whence they spring, into the Mediterranean Sea near Narbonne. She exhales. Part of her is tired. To be continued. For now the feeling of being the right size in the right place will do very well. She gives thanks.

Paulita's Story

A Home in France

I didn't fall in love with France after my first visit – although I did lose my virginity. I went on one of those 21-day, 28-country bus tours with other university students, and my then boyfriend. We looked at engagement rings during our brief stop in Luxembourg, leaning toward the Princess Diana sapphire surrounded by diamonds as we dreamed about a future life together back in the U.S. When we found ourselves alone in a hotel in Paris, all the other students on the tour out exploring the city, we had sex for the first time. But discarded virginity doesn't guarantee a lifelong obsession with a place.

The relationship didn't last, but my interest in France was piqued. I'd studied French in high school, and I minored in French in college. Another boyfriend is the one who got me hooked on France because his connections helped me secure a three-month gig as an au pair. His sister was married to a Frenchman. They lived in the U.S. and had two little girls, ages three and four, plus a third child on the way. They had planned to go to France the summer of 1986, but the mother began to have difficulties with her pregnancy. The parents decided to send the girls to France for the summer to be with their French grandparents. Since the grandparents were well into their 70s, the parents felt an au pair was a necessity to help care for the kids. I quickly volunteered, telling my city editor at the local newspaper that I was taking a leave of absence for the summer and waving goodbye to the photographer boyfriend who had made the connections for me – something he probably regretted since I broke up with him the day I returned from France.

I enjoyed shepherding the little girls around Paris for a few days before we flew to Corsica and spent a month in a stone house, taking daily forays to the beach and sitting down to huge meals each evening. I dressed in swirling skirts and kitten heels with lacy socks, á la Madonna. I sailed on the Mediterranean and saw flying fish for the first time and basked in the sun while reading F. Scott Fitzgerald. I averted my eyes when we visited a naturist beach, and I discovered that most French men are not circumcised. I learned which cheeses to eat with which wines under the careful tutelage of a French doctor, uncle to the girls. But all of it seemed like a temporary vacation until we visited Aix en Provence.

We had left Corsica and would drive across France to Bourges, where the family had a vacation manor since the time of Napoleon. These grandparents did not want an au pair along. They much preferred to have control of their own granddaughters with no interference. Their muttering in French mostly went unnoticed by me, but I could feel the malevolence.

Our first night driving, we stopped at their relative's house in Aix en Provence. It is known as the city of fountains and was first settled by the Romans. It has a lovely wide avenue called the Cours Mirabeau with four fountains dotting the street and upscale shops and more down-to-earth restaurants. The relative, sensing the grandparents' displeasure with me, offered to take me out to see the city. She would get me out of the grandparents' hair for a few hours. As we walked the Cours Mirabeau, stopping at various shops, I felt a pang inside. I realized I'd been here before. Not in this life, but something told me I'd come home. Maybe I was here as a Roman. Or a Visigoth. Or as a French man or woman in the 12th century when Aix en Provence's artistic scene began to flourish. Perhaps it was much more recent, like the late 1800s when Paul Cezanne painted impressionist paintings of Mt. Saint Victoire, the mountain that loomed outside of town. Whenever I might have made my home in Aix en Provence, my heart recognized it and clicked, like a puzzle piece, completing the whole. I was home.

France put a crowbar in my brain and opened it up to so many new experiences. The joy of sitting on a stone terrace overlooking the

Mediterranean while someone passionately played the piano. The taste of fresh nectarine juice and the feeling of its ripeness dripping down my chin. The awe of seeing tapestries hundreds of years old, with each colorful stitch conscientiously looped through the fabric as it continued to add color and life to cold walls.

After three months as an au pair, I flew back to the States with the little girls so they could meet their new baby brother. And I returned with a passion to learn everything I could. To read every book. To play every song. To stitch every tapestry. And most of all, to return to France to experience a passion for life.

Thirty-two years later, I prepared to move to France with my husband Earl. He wasn't the photographer boyfriend with French connections. Instead, he was just a boy from Ohio, who I met while we both worked as journalists at a newspaper in Florida. We'd taken a circuitous route to find each other. I took him on his first trip to France. We went back twice with the kids and snuck in visits just the two of us. He fell for the country as hard as I did.

Moving to France had long been a dream that Earl and I discussed, something we speculated about when our three kids were young, and we first took them overseas. Could we move to France, find jobs and raise our kids there? What about a bed & breakfast, we speculated, not knowing how clichéd the idea was with thousands of English-speakers moving to France to make a life owning a gite. Again, as the kids hit their adolescence and we saw the years ticking past, we speculated on whether moving to France was a possibility, but back then we never took the steps to make it a reality.

Our long-term plan had always been to retire to France. Earl's father, all his uncles, and his brother had heart troubles that started in their fifties. Earl insisted he would retire at sixty-two so he could enjoy life before the inevitable happened. Our family relied on Earl's job for health insurance, and since I am seven years younger than him, I'd have to wait even longer for government health coverage. But if we retired to France, we could pay for French health coverage at less than a tenth of the cost.

I'd always insisted that if we moved to France, we needed to keep a house in the U.S., some place the kids could call home, where they could drop in and feel the stress of the world lift from their shoulders, like I do when I walk into my parents' house. But if we bought a new home in Ohio, we couldn't afford a place in France. So we hesitated.

A note from my Aunt Esther helped change my mind.

The last time I had seen Aunt Esther, I told her my latest novel was about two women hiking the Appalachian Trail; her eyes got round behind her glasses.

Oh, that's my thing! she said.

So I sent her the book that week, and the following week, I got a note from her, along with a cheque to repay me for the book. Aunt Esther turned ninety in 2015. She had married my mother's oldest brother, Uncle Junior, who fought in World War II in Italy. But their story of romance during wartime wasn't what inspired me in the note. She wrote to thank me for my book *Trail Mix* and for the opportunity to go on the adventure. She had always wanted to hike the Appalachian Trail.

Aunt Esther wrote: *I let time run out on my DREAM to hike the Trail.* She told me about the times she had walked on snippets of the trail, at the trail head in north Georgia, across the Blue Ridge Highway, at the top of Old Man Mountain in Vermont. *Last, we made it to the beginning of the end (or beginning of the Trail). We hiked to within an hour of the summit the Ranger told us. We came to a boulder too much for us to get over.*

I felt Aunt Esther's pain of a dream that had slipped away.

My other dream was to walk the Grand Canyon. But Old Mother Nature's Clock just went too fast, she wrote.

And it struck me: how fast would those years go by and how many regrets would we have? If we bought a house in France, we could always sell it to buy another place in Ohio if we wanted to come back. And so, I said to Earl, *We can move to France when you retire at sixty-two.*

In May 2016, just eighteen months before Earl's retirement, I sat at the end of our long farmhouse table facing the open kitchen. The living room behind me was open to the dining room, and the British voices of the soccer commentators provided background for my typing. We hadn't turned any lights on as the bright sun reflected into the room, knowing the temperature was forecast to climb to nearly ninety that day. But the front porch sheltered the living room from direct light. The room where I sat felt womb-like, dim, yet I faced the gleaming outdoors through the windows and the glass storm door. The air conditioning cooled me. The morning sports broadcast from Europe hummed in the background like a summer tradition. I sipped a latte – decaf. I realized that I wanted to keep feeling like that forever – comfortable, safe in a house that we loved in the community we loved.

But in less than two years, we wouldn't be there. We wouldn't have that house with the big front porch that perched at the top of a hill and gave a panoramic view of downtown Columbus, at least in the winter when the trees' leaves fell.

Suddenly, I had cold feet.

Earl and I discussed the budget. So many unknowns hovered above our heads. How much would we earn on the sale of the house? Would I be able to get a job in France or would there be online classes I could teach from my current colleges? Would my books be selling and bringing in a steady income?

Our life and plans tipped like a teeter totter from one side to the other. Jubilation and joy at the idea of exploring Europe, fear that we'd throw away all the things we loved and come limping home. One thing I knew, my husband planned to retire, which meant our life would change, whether in the United States or in France. The life in the U.S. was the one I knew. Our house with its squeaky, squeaky floors. The bedroom with triple windows across the front wall. Shutters covered the bottom of the windows so the light poured in from the top. During the autumn and the spring, the light from a full moon would burrow into my sleeping eyes and wake me. I'd blink in the brightness and wonder that the moon had returned to that same place where it could peer in my window, illuminating the bare tree branches.

Sometimes, our house resembled a tree house. The view out the front windows consisted of leaves and branches. In the spring, for a week, the flowering plum tree would be covered with tiny white flowers. When I walked in the back door and saw the blossoming tree through the front window, I would momentarily think it was snowing out front before I realized that the tree caused the apparent snowstorm.

In the backyard, we had a fairly large swathe of grass with a sidewalk that led to the garage. The backyard offered a brown metal table and chairs with a large green umbrella open to protect the table from the sun. A green hammock swayed in the grass next to a wooden Adirondack chair that I had found abandoned by the road one year. I carried it home over my head and painted it white. Along the edge of the yard, we had a bed of strawberries, a bed of raspberries, and a raised garden where we grew tomatoes and lettuce. Sometimes, we splurged with cucumbers or green beans. Earl had even experimented with mounds of potatoes and stalks of asparagus.

The small house in a cozy community just seemed like home. I couldn't imagine not having it – not having a place for the kids to come if they'd lost a job or had a breakup or if they just wanted to hang out and watch a sporting event.

I wished we could keep it and buy a house in France. I knew the dangers of a safety net though. If things got tough in France, I'd consider running back to my familiar house in Ohio. Plus, as a newspaperman and an adjunct professor, we weren't the two-house kind of family.

In the summers, we frequently turned on European sports, watching the Tour de France, Wimbledon, and European soccer.

Next year, we'll be watching the Tour in person, I reminded Earl one day.
Yep.

And it will be in the afternoon. That'll be weird, won't it?
He agreed.

Moving to France would be a big risk – everything would change. But we did it. As Earl turned sixty-two, he retired. We closed on the sale of the house. We spent a last Christmas together with the kids and my parents in Florida, and we moved to France. We had our visas, secured from the Chicago office. We had housesits for the first few months. We would play it by ear.

Those first days in Paris seemed idyllic. The plane arrived in France earlier than scheduled. We scurried through the airport hallways and arrived at passport check. I handed the customs agent my passport open to the correct page and then flipped to the page with the visa.
J'ai un visa, aussi, I told him, I have a visa, too.
Ah, oui? his eyebrows shot up. Americans can visit European countries for ninety days without a visa, so most Americans come simply armed with a passport. The agent stamped the page opposite my visa and Earl's too.

Once we'd gathered our bags, seven in total counting carry-ons and personal items, we wheeled them through customs without being stopped and were met by Andre our driver holding a phone with my name printed on it. We apologized for the number of bags and he waved us off. He had a big car, he assured us. And he did -- one of those van/delivery truck vehicles. We usually wrangled our suitcases on the train and chugged into the city, but with so much luggage, we had decided to reserve a ride. Andre made short work of our giant suitcases and drove through the awakening city.

I could have simply sat in the car looking dreamily at the hotel glowing in the early winter morning. Groups of warm yellow lights draped the bushes that lined the marble walkway. Potted green pines shone with more lights on either side of the front door, and another blanket of lights hung from a small balcony above the door. After Andre deposited us at the hotel, just a few streets from Notre Dame and Shakespeare and Co. bookstore, the hotel upgraded our room so we could fit all of our big suitcases inside.

At that time of the morning, our room wasn't ready. We knew we had a day full of activities to get through before we could settle into bed to take a nap. Starting the adventure of a new life in France meant that adrenaline and sheer giddiness would keep us going for a while.

While in Paris we rode Le Grand Roue, the giant Ferris Wheel, to enjoy the lights. We had a wine and cheese tour. We visited markets and ate pastries. One night as we returned to the hotel, my hand clasped in Earl's I breathed in the beautiful sights, Christmas tree lights glistening in front of government buildings, stores shimmering with twinkling colors. Paris decorated for the Christmas season was something to behold. How had we never done it before?

The glow from a restaurant pulled us in. It looked so cozy. A man stood outside shucking oysters, his breath steaming in the cold. Steak and frites for me. A few more glasses of wine before stumbling back to the room.

This dream, this chance we took on moving to France, it was all worth it. Our entire life had become a fairytale. As we traveled throughout France, doing housesits in the Charente, scurrying over to England for a few weeks, then back to France for a stay along the Atlantic coast and finally settling in Aix en Provence for six weeks, we had a chance to compare the different areas and determine if the region we planned to move to was right for us.

We'd chosen the southwest of France, toward Spain and along the Pyrenees, but also within an hour of the Mediterranean. It seemed to have everything – mountains for hiking, the sea for swimming, and inexpensive housing. We loved the Provence region, but the housing costs were much higher there.

The spring before we moved, we'd done a reconnaissance mission, visiting about ten towns in a two week period to check out their markets. We had a list of necessary things in our future home town. A market was one of those things. We also wanted the town to have restaurants and cafés, along with a grocery within walking distance since we didn't plan to get a car right away. As we traveled from one stunning town to another, this one with a chateau and that one with a Medieval town center, I began to wonder how we would choose. We narrowed it down to two towns – Quillan with a population of about 3,000 sitting in a bowl of mountains, and Pezenas with a population of about 8,000 and closer to the sea.

After we moved to France, we spent a week in each town. In Quillan, we hardly had time to search for apartments to rent because we would set out hiking each morning or go to the market on Wednesdays and Saturdays to enjoy a coffee in the restaurant along the river, watching flowers sprout from the stones that made up the old bridge. We knew no English speakers except for the Australian owners of the B&B, but they offered lots of advice about moving to Quillan.

Standing in Quillan, surrounded by mountains, some high and jutting stones into the sky, some more rounded and covered with the deep green of pine trees, it felt like a giant hug, like the mountains would keep me safe. In the evenings, the sun would turn those pale rocks pink. I loved the view of the moon peeking over the peaks or the sun slowly sinking between the mountains.

In our search for an apartment rental, we tried the real estate agents who sent us to the tourism office. The tourism office had a list of addresses and phone numbers, many of them out of date. We saw a few apartments, but none that were furnished or had kitchens. In the U.S., every apartment or house comes with a kitchen. In France, apparently people move their kitchens with them whether renting or buying. We hesitated to spend money on a kitchen for an apartment where we might live for only six months.

Just before we left town, we heard about a house for rent from May through December. A visit to the three-bedroom house with large garden seemed just right for us. The rent was 800 euros but they dropped it to 700 euros if Earl would do the yard work. We told them we'd let them know after our week-long stay in Pezenas.

Driving from Quillan to Pezenas felt like a big change. From a mountain town to a seaside town. Maybe it was leaving behind the comfort of the mountains in the Aude, or perhaps, having seen a comfortable house and imagining myself living there through the end of the year, but something made me a bit resentful as we drove the two hours to Pezenas and pulled in.

The stone staircase of the Airbnb curved around to the spacious apartment. The gracious hostess met us at the historic edge of the town and pushed the button for the roadblocks to descend so that we could wind our rental car through narrow cobblestoned streets. We parked in front of her garage door as she assured us that she would be able to negotiate her Harley Davidson around the car.

We went walking through Pezenas. With my stomach still full from lunch at a restaurant along the route, I wasn't temped by the *patisseries*, the *boulangeries*, the *salons de thé*, or the many restaurants. And, although we stopped to *lèche-vitrines* (window shop, but it literally means lick the windows) at many immobiliers, I dreaded trying to negotiate in French-English with the real estate agents and schlepping to look at apartments that don't come with kitchens.

Instead, I pictured that house in Quillan that we had viewed, with the wood beams across the living room ceiling and the veranda outside the kitchen, sun from three sides and a nice stone patio where we could sit in the summer to catch the breeze blowing down from the mountains.
I felt resentful.

Was there nothing to do in this town but eat and buy property? I wondered.

We passed a theater where a crowd had gathered, but we'd been to see a movie in English with French subtitles the night before. We hoped we were close enough to the Mediterranean Sea to ride bikes there, but all the bicycle places we tried to contact didn't open until tourist season.

We spent the evening in, reading books since the WiFi connection wasn't strong enough to stream Netflix. My unease with the city grew. I kept thinking, *I'm not living my best life.* Maybe it had to do with the amount of time I had to do anything I wanted – or nothing. If I was home in Ohio, I'd have been teaching six classes. As I traveled, I only had one class. Again, I felt my dream drifting away from me. Had I been wrong to give up everything and move to France? I always thought I was the adventurous type, but now I dreaded going to talk to real estate agents. The next morning, I messaged a friend who held my secrets close and told her about my fears. Then I circled down the stone staircase and let my feet explore the town.

After a five-mile run augmented by uplifting music, I walked toward the old city and our apartment. I paused to read a plaque on a building and noticed that it was a bakery with no customers inside, a perfect opportunity for me since I didn't want to offend people with my sweatiness. I ducked inside and bought croissants for our breakfast. The woman inside commented - in a friendly way - on my run, my *sportif* activities, and I smiled and agreed that it allowed me to eat more. We both laughed and I continued on my way, following the map to our stone apartment where my husband awaited to let me in the locked doors, living a life that I had chosen, promising to make my dreams come true.

As our week in Pezenas wound down, I realized I owed an apology to the town after saying that the only thing there were *boulangeries* and real estate agents. As I explored, I realized that the town is a great supporter of artists. The whole place was full of *ateliers* – workshops for artists. Not many of them were open in February, but I could definitely see how tourists would love to visit and just saunter through the village, watching the artists and buying things to take home.

Since my move to France, I'd had some tough days, and it felt so wimpy to say that I was unhappy in France, but lots of times, *happily ever after* didn't come without some pitfalls.

In May, we filled our car with all of our suitcases, hung our bicycles off the back of the car on a bike carrier, and headed for southwestern France. We had chosen the rental house in Quillan.

Each morning, we would throw open the shutters and admire the view of the mountains that surrounded us. We would run and hike. We made friends, mostly English speakers, but a few French speakers, and we started to adjust to life in rural France. We would traipse into town to meet friends at the market, stopping at the *boulangerie* for a croissant or a chocolatine (as our part of France calls a pain au chocolat). The baker would soon come from his kitchen to offer me cheek kisses and urged me to tutoyer him (use the familiar form of you). We followed leaders along the path for a night hike that ended in a meal in the town meeting room. And as we drank the aperitif, wine and pastis, they set up speakers. After the meal, we danced with abandon until we spilled from the room after midnight and walked back to our rental house in the dark holding hands.

After five years in France, we've learned to close our shutters against the too hot sun in July and to throw them open at night to welcome the cool night breeze into the house with its thick stone walls. We know to buy supplies for a Sunday dinner on Saturday, because all of the stores will be closed Sunday afternoon. We have discovered which days cafés are open and which days they are closed and have adjusted our schedules. We still get a bit frustrated that the hardware store closes from 12-2 everyday, but who are we to say that a 2-hour lunch isn't a priority.

After the rental house that first year, we bought a house of our own with a small garden that each year features sunflowers that stretch above the fence as if peering at the people who walk past.

Nothing in life is perfect, but we have snippets of perfection throughout our days or weeks or months. We live a life that is filled with sensory moments, like the smell of lavender that wafts in my door now and the buzz of the bees stopping for a few moments on the pale purple flowers. And we know we belong in this part of France surrounded by the mountains and the sound of now familiar French voices.

Tina's Story

August 2023

Lying on my back on the swimming pool deck, looking at the night sky. Countless sparkling stars in the heavens; there appears to be layer upon layer of stars stretching into infinity. I am hoping to see the Perseid meteor shower. I wait for an hour or so and can hear the sounds of the night, an infrequent car passing on the road and the chirping of the cicadas. The noise of the river flowing behind the house. After spotting a few satellites following their orbits, I notice a movement in the sky in my peripheral vision. I switch position and focus on where I think the movement has originated. About fifteen minutes later I am rewarded by a magnificent tailed meteor streaking across the sky. Several more appear, some with tails and some without. There's something very magical about being here, I feel incredibly connected with nature. The sky above my house provides daytime opportunities for observations of the natural world. In the daytime the sight of vultures wheeling around above me is awe inspiring. The sound of nightingales singing at night in late spring, the buzzing of the bumblebees on the lavender as well as rumbling thunder on summer days provide an opportunity for connection I didn't have in my old life. The gentle rhythm of the changing seasons as well as the occasional violence of storms and strong winds remind me of the force of Mother Nature. Ultimately this is partly why I have found my forever home in this part of France. I feel connected to the landscape and feel far more *myself* here than I have anywhere else.

My journey to Quillan has been a long one! But I finally feel I've arrived home.

It was 2015. I had four children, was about to turn fifty and had ended a long marriage and moved from Kings Langley to a smaller house in St Albans, Hertfordshire about a twenty minute drive away. I was keen to keep disruption for the family to a minimum so there was no fighting for a fair split of assets, it was important for me that the younger children remained at their school. Naively I thought the children would not be impacted massively by the split but ultimately there were certainly repercussions that I had not foreseen and the younger children were negatively affected. Care of my two younger children was shared with my ex-husband, the two older children living independently. Life took on a different rhythm.

Work took up a lot of time but it was important for me and my training had been expensive and arduous. I had begun training as a counsellor when I was thirty-eight after my youngest son had started nursery school. My previous career had been a mental health nurse, working in a psychiatric intensive care unit in north west London. As well as a year working as a drug and alcohol counsellor in a prison and in the community, sandwiched in the middle. I didn't really enjoy this role. The charity I worked for had significant organisational issues and I didn't like being incarcerated for long periods of the day. I went back to the familiar NHS role within the same team. It would seem that I didn't like change back then. Also childcare for shift work was an awful lot cheaper than 9 to 5 childcare.

I wasn't ambitious when I worked in the NHS and achieved the dizzying heights of deputy ward manager. I think I had too much headspace taken up with bringing up children. I left the world of the psychiatric intensive care unit when my youngest son was born in 2000. There had been a couple of incidents involving a lot of blood and violence (neither mine) that had resulted in a burn out of sorts.

The following three years of domesticity reinforced that I wasn't really a very good housewife so I decided to retrain in the field of counselling. Training and working at Relate was a revelation; most of the clientele actually wanted some help/support, not requiring restraint (physical or chemical) or a lock and key. I enjoyed the work and the studying was interesting. I could see a career path that felt both exciting and useful. After completing my post graduate certificate in couple counselling I started the two year training to qualify as a psychosexual therapist. It seemed to me that relationships and sex were utterly intertwined and to offer help for one without the other was fruitless.

After completing the post graduate diploma in psychosexual therapy I enrolled on the two year Master's programme. Having never gone to university as a school leaver (due to incredibly poor A level results) this felt momentous. My twenty thousand word dissertation was about how therapists managed a couple treatment plan where there were differing libidos.

Then it was on to the next challenge, seemingly my ambition had been liberated!

After completing the master's degree in psychosexual therapy I successfully applied for a job I saw advertised for the local sexual health centre. This was a somewhat disappointing time, despite managing to get the job amidst fierce competition. I was working alone in a role that the department really didn't seem to want. I was not a doctor as the previous incumbent had been, so I frequently needed to refer clients to the doctors within the sexual health centre for physical investigations. I lasted four years, by which time frequent no shows (it turns out that people don't seem to value something they can have for nothing) and an inability to see clients for the necessary length of time (I was limited to six sessions as opposed to at least twelve in the private sector), resulted in a dulling of my satisfaction with the role. When the sexual health department was taken over by a private provider, my role wasn't featured on any personnel flow charts. It seemed to me that the time to leave was upon me and I could focus on private practice.

Private practice was building up so I didn't really notice the loss of income from the NHS. I had continued studying while working in the NHS, completing a year's training in working with clients who had sexual addiction and compulsivity. Ultimately, this was an area of work I did not enjoy. The clients (mostly male) had a different type of need to my regular client group. Sometimes they presented for therapy under duress having been discovered using porn or escort services by their partners. In these instances therapy was rarely effective, as they didn't really want to change. Rarely I worked with clients who wanted to change. That would have been much more fulfilling.

My next piece of training was a bit more unusual. This coincided with the end of my marriage, I think I must have been on a 'journey' of sorts.

Some experiential training days in tantric practices had resulted in me looking towards a more holistic approach to therapy. One that required a move towards less conventional practices. I found a course that appealed and despite the expense, I started a new training, hoping to incorporate new skills into my practice. My cohort on the training included tantric sex workers as well as conventional psychotherapists. Ultimately I didn't finish the course. It felt like I was on a path that didn't feel entirely comfortable. 'Cuddle puddles' and orgasmic meditation were not the answer I was looking for.

So, I was single and fifty. What next?

I had been online dating following the end of my marriage and after a fruitless year of inappropriate matches and dates I met Nick. Our fourth date was in a vineyard in Tuscany. I knew he was a keeper!!

Nick proposed in Place Carnot in Carcassonne, France on New Year's Day 2017. His father had gone to the restaurant's restroom.

Nick had bought a motorhome, we had used it a few times in the UK for weekends. We were living in separate places an hour apart. He was in Bedfordshire in a sweet old cottage, and I was in St Alban's. We planned a trip to France in July 2017. His dad lives in St Hilaire close to Limoux and we decided to head there. Before the trip we had spent a little time looking at property for sale in the area. We had talked about wanting to live elsewhere and had both seen a house we liked the look of in Quillan. This had then been pushed to the back of our minds as a bit of harmless fantasy.

We headed to France with our two dogs: Storm, a retriever and Scruff, a large labradoodle. We spent a few days meandering through France, stopping wherever the mood took us and exploring beautiful countryside.

Upon arriving in St Hilaire we thought it might be interesting to look at some houses and test the water. We arranged a viewing for the house we had seen online. Upon arriving at the gates of the house and looking down the drive I think I fell in love. But I couldn't allow myself to become attached to the idea, this isn't what we had planned. It was too soon into our relationship and although we were engaged we weren't living together.

We were shown around the house and gardens by the Spanish couple who owned it. They were very proud of their blue bathroom with Aphrodite depicted on the tiles. I continued to try and stay grounded. Part of me was becoming excited by the possibilities. The other part was focussed on being sensible.

There was a small river running behind the house and the property was nestled between two hills covered with green oak. At the back of the house was a dilapidated old mill building and to the right was a small wooded area with chickens scratching in the earth behind the woodshed. The grounds at the front had been used to grow produce; potatoes, strawberry plants and globe artichokes could be seen in the field. The other side of the garden had fruit trees; apple, fig, cherry, pear and two mystery trees that I later learnt were quince and persimmon.

The crazy paved terrace to the left-hand side led out to a lawn, accessed under an orange trumpet vine in full bloom. A gate to the side of the upper garden led to a path running along the edge of the river. It felt idyllic and I fell under the house's spell.

We left the viewing and I was feeling confused. The house and land were amazing but was it all possible in reality?

That afternoon we visited another house that was an old trout farm in the mountains. We both felt the trout farm was too far from civilisation and potentially dark in winter so we discounted the only other runner.

Nick put his cottage in Bedfordshire on the market as soon as we arrived back and an offer was made on the house in Quillan. The first offer was rejected, the second accepted.

Nerves kicked in, was it the right decision or just a poorly thought through impulsive daydream?

Nick's cottage sold quickly, and we were able to proceed with buying the house in Quillan, with some financial aid from his mum.

I assumed that Quillan was an area with few English speakers, (I don't have any idea how I came to this erroneous belief) and imagined that my extremely limited grasp of the French language would improve as if by osmosis just by spending time here.

When we came back to France in December for the completion of the paperwork for the sale, I realised, as we sat in *Les Platanes* restaurant one evening, celebrating our purchase, that the majority of the clientele were English speakers. It was early December and not holiday season. The penny dropped! The fact there were English speaking residents was actually reassuring. It meant we were not the only ones to fall in love with this special place.

And as for learning French (shrug) that would just take a bit longer!

The next few months included frequent trips to Quillan, overseeing the construction of the pool, juggling work and parenting responsibilities. There were three weddings in 2018; my second son's, my eldest son's and then mine! One of my children still lived at home and was attending a local college. Two had flown the nest sometime earlier and one was studying at university. All were supportive of our decision to buy a holiday home and the potential plan of us moving to France full time eventually.

I remember feeling very excited before our trips down to Quillan, whether we flew or drove. I had a sense of coming home. In all the other places I had lived, I felt like each home was a stepping stone, temporary, and not where I felt relaxed.

Quillan felt very different.

Of course there were challenges: language being the primary difficulty. I had abandoned languages at school by the age of thirteen. My mum is a Francophile and the rebel in me had decided French was not cool. If only I'd listened to my mum. I started learning French before we made the move over. A lovely French woman called Aurora came to our house once a week in St Albans. Nick was also having lessons with her but his French was more advanced than mine so we had separate lessons.

So for a couple of years we spent holidays in Quillan, renovating our home, enjoying the different seasons and the different pace of life.

Brexit forced us to commit to living full time in France. For that I will be eternally grateful. The only good thing to come out of the mess it has become. We were both able to wind down our businesses.

I was ready to retire and Nick was too.

We moved permanently in October 2019, making the journey down in a left hand drive Belgian registered car we had bought in the U.K. Accompanying us were two dogs and a cat. We missed our crossing on Eurostar due to a last minute panic over full bins (and where to abandon them) in our St Albans house. Sitting in the Euro Tunnel departure car park with pots and pans on my knee with five hours to wait for the next available crossing, I decided to fill the nearest bin with these items. The thought of pots and pans on my lap for a further thirteen hours was unbearable. The car was rammed with our possessions and pets. Due to the delay the journey required an unplanned overnight stop in Limoges. We smuggled the cat in to the hotel, having declared the dogs and didn't want to push our luck.

Arriving at our permanent home felt wonderful. My husband's father had been working on our dark, dusty space downstairs to make it usable as a holiday rental property for the following summer. There was a lot of work needed to get the rest of the house ready, but we decided to do it room by room.

Our first Christmas was spent in the U.K. as my first grandchild had recently been born. The tug of family in the U.K. has been an ongoing theme that was intensified as covid began to spread throughout the world. Transport to the U.K. became impossible and seeing loved ones likewise. However that first summer all my children and grandson made it over to France despite the changing rules and border closures, for a truly memorable fortnight.

Also in 2020 we tried renting out the renovated apartment below our living accommodation. We rented it out for five weeks in total. The first guests were a Belgian family with two teenage boys. The boys drained our alcohol optics (apart from the one containing Pastis) and then blocked our drains. The second family were French and had a young boy and a dog. These guests had to endure the consequences of the drains blocked by the previous guests.

We discovered that we really didn't enjoy hosting and we were not comfortable with being in such close proximity to other people. We spent a lot of the summer inside our house while our guests enjoyed the pool, outside kitchen and gardens. Lesson learnt!

Another lesson we learnt was not to buy an old property. As we had decided not to rent out our apartment we thought we might need a different income stream. So we purchased an old two bedroom village house about twenty minutes away with the intention of renting this out for holidays. Far enough to not be in close proximity to us but near enough to be able to maintain it and complete changeovers. As I write this, over two years later, the renovation is still not finished and the house is realistically about a year from being completed. There are many reasons we have not achieved our goal but chiefly it seems that we have become accustomed to not doing a great deal and enjoying our life in France.

Our two dogs who made the original journey to view the house have since died. One was put to sleep due to old age and poor health, the other died suddenly two days later (maybe a broken heart). Nick needed a dog so within a week we had a rescue dog with many issues. He remains a work in progress!

The things I love about France primarily involve the lifestyle. This part of France seems to understand the notion of a work life balance. Most shops, apart from the supermarket, shut for two hours at lunchtime. The pace of life is slower.

The emphasis on good local food is significant, although I miss vegetarian options being mainstream, and having to hunt around for halloumi or tahini can become frustrating.

I love the lack of materialism, the notion of having to *keep up with the Jones's* doesn't exist in the same way as the U.K. Old bangers frequent the roads and clothes don't have to be up to the minute high fashion.

I value the friendships I have made here, with women of a similar age who have emigrated to France. In a sense the difficulties with covid enabled these friendships to be nurtured as outside considerations were limited. The fellow English speaking residents of the town are a friendly bunch, some have an interest in alternative health and spirituality which I am becoming more drawn to.

I love the dramatic scenery in this part of the world; the mountains, lakes and plateaus, how the seasons change and life's activities follow the seasons.

As two more grandchildren have arrived since the first in 2019, and another is on the way; the pull of family remains. My mother is eighty and very healthy and robust at the moment, but I am aware this may change in the future. I have decided to cross that bridge when necessary.

For now, I try to live in the moment, exploring creative avenues and meditating. Finding enjoyment in a simpler way of life and working on improving my poor French. In the words of Edith Piaf, *Non, je ne regrette rien.*

Mischa's Story

Have you ever smelled something that reminds you of a time and place or an experience that's really familiar? It happens to me now and then and, years later, sometimes it is so vivid that it stops me in my tracks and transports me back to my childhood in Africa. I remember the smell of the red earth following a long awaited rainstorm, the sweet scent of creamy frangipani flowers, the sickly smell of ripe pawpaw at breakfast, cedar wood burning on a mountain hut fire, pungent, leathery tobacco leaves hanging in the barn, fish drying on racks in the sunshine, fly-infested meat at the local market, and overcrowded buses with chickens panting and squawking and fragrant, sweaty armpits on a hot day. Senses and memories always connecting us to our surroundings.

Around me now are spectacular sunsets, morning mist rising to reveal dramatic, impressive mountain peaks, deep imposing jagged gorges, spectacular waterfalls, the same brown and white spotted hoopoes, the smell of fermenting grape skins at the end of a busy harvest. Familiarities that stop me and cause me to reflect. This is my story, my chapter of how I migrated to live in Quillan, France.

Travel has always featured strongly in my family. My mum, who is Dutch, was born in Indonesia and relocated, as a refugee after the war, to Holland. She met my dad, from Barnsley, Yorkshire, whilst volunteering following an earthquake in Morocco. In 1962 they married in Holland. My mum was eight months pregnant when they flew to Kenya where my dad started a teaching job. My brother Alrik was born in a bush clinic in Kaimosi on the edge of Lake Victoria. The generator had broken down so the only lights shining in were car headlights! Two years later on 1st July 1966, I was born in much the same way! Two years after me my sister, Anja-Maaike, was born in Haverhill, England, and three years after that we moved back to Africa, to Malawi where my younger brother Frans was born. Now we were four.

In *Out of Africa* Isak Dinesan famously begins her story *I had a farm in Africa, at the foot of the Ngong hills.* In Malawi we did live at the foot of Soche Hill, then the foot of Zomba plateau and now I live at the foot of the Pyrenees in France. We didn't have a farm, well not exactly. It was more a menagerie of found and rescued animals. I was an animal obsessed child as you will see.

I remember our first house, the one at the foot of Soche Hill had a large animal enclosure and nearly every night a pack of hyaenas would descend the hill and enter our garden looking for scraps to eat. I would lie in bed listening to the hideous laughing getting closer and closer. They would squabble among themselves as they overturned and rummaged through the bins. For many fearful nights I slept at the end of my parent's bed thus creating my loathing for hyaenas. I also remember my brother and I being off school with hepatitis and sitting under the table giggling and blissfully snipping away at each other's hair. Our daft dog, Trumpet, would follow our VW Combi for miles and I remember our other dog, Cleo, went missing for three days and was eventually found in the woods with her leg in a snare. Mum saved her leg and nursed her back to health. I also recall our VW Combi, crammed with twelve children on the way to school ,and the day it descended into a ditch, nearly keeling over with us scrambling around in a heap – you can imagine the excitement.

You may be sensing by now that my childhood was far from ordinary, definitely unconventional and was filled with adventure and experiences that most children couldn't possibly imagine. To me this was just normal life. Television didn't exist in Malawi so we had to create our own entertainment. We were rarely in the house and would disappear, usually barefoot, on our bikes, and would come home only when driven back by hunger at the close of day. We had complete freedom but we also needed to learn how to be safe. A favourite day for us was to clamber up the potato path that ran behind our house at the foothill to the top of Zomba plateau. On the way we would run up and down this enormous sawdust pile at the sawmill then carry on up, pockets filled with fragrant, warm wood chippings. We knew we were about half way up when we reached the tree with the leopard scratches on it! We would build dams or fill a bucket with crabs caught with bacon rind bait and string. Perhaps this was the start of my love of mountains and water.

We all loved swimming and spent endless hours in the outdoor pool at our school, shadowed majestically by Zomba plateau. We also spent many holidays at Lake Malawi, a jewel with its beautiful clear water, tangly weeds, and abundant, vividly coloured chichlid fish, as well as crocodiles and hippos. The water was so clear that, as we swam to Otter Point, which was a very long swim, we would look down to see the giant circular hippo prints in the sediment below. This made us swim a bit faster! Local fishermen in precarious dug-out canoes would paddle the shores selling their catch of the day. Once I spent my pocket money on a giant catfish which we put in the bath to recover. It had string through its gills and was so big that my brother rode it into the lake before cutting the string to set it free. Great memories for a wild child.

I was mad on animals. A few times a year, and as a special treat, dad would rent films from the British Council. He would rig up the big reel projector aimed at the white wall in the sitting room and all our little feral friends would come to our cinema. My favourite film that I always requested was *The Migration of the Caribou*. It fascinated me - a bit like the migration of the wildebeest in the Masai Mara but with snow. We had never seen snow. A short Woody Woodpecker film would follow but this was always in high demand and not always available.

I was often in trouble when I was at school. I was late most mornings, usually because I got side tracked walking down the rocky stream path to school. In my satchel was possibly a snakeskin, a birds' or hornets' nest, bones, skulls, dead beetles or feathers. I would collect for the nature table in our classroom. It was a big table! I managed to hide some chameleon eggs in my desk but trouble began when they hatched and were crawling out of the ink hole. This lead to yet another bum whack with Sir's tennis shoe (tackie) in his office. There was never a dull moment... I could write a book!

We always had dogs and cats but gradually this increased to a quite bizarre collection of creatures. I tried to rescue anything that needed rescuing. My sister and I did a sponsored swim then spent the money we collected saving 'Donald' the duck from his demise in the cooking pot. I would save all my tambala pocket money just in case. Sometimes children would sell animals on the roadside. I knew it was wrong, but I couldn't resist, so we ended up with a hedgehog (Horace) and a baby baboon (Babsie) to add to our existing mini zoo of ducks, guinea pigs, rabbits, a leather-shelled green turtle, bantam chickens (that would walk through the house and across the piano keys), numerous birds, a white rat (aptly named Billy Big Balls that we rescued from the university laboratory), a leopard tortoise and my sheep, Hugo, who was given to me because I was so brave and got back on a horse after falling off. I loved riding and my sister and I would ride bareback playing *cowboys n injuns* charging around our friend's tobacco farm. We found three crocodile eggs buried in the sand at the lake and brought them home with us. We always had a lightbulb lit inside the piano to stop the humidity sticking down the keys. We filled a large Nestlé dried milk tin with sand, burying the eggs and hovered the light bulb over it. Eventually the eggs hatched and the three snappy baby crocodiles caused a great deal of excitement. We couldn't keep them for obvious reasons!

My tenth birthday was approaching. There was a big build up to my birthday present. Mum would say things like *It is very tall, will need looking after and you will have it for a long time.* Well that was it... I was beyond excited, thinking I was getting a baby giraffe. Our enclosure might need to be adapted a bit. I had never wanted anything as much as this. My birthday arrived and, blindfolded, I was led to my present. I couldn't feel a neck sticking out and it was very thin. Unwrapping it revealed a big, green metal adult bicycle. I was so disappointed. I never could reach the pedals properly.

Given all this wildness, it's hard to imagine I went to ballet lessons. Each week my dedicated mum would drive miles to my class for which I had two incentives for going. The first of which was being treated to a huge Knickerbocker Glory from the ice cream parlour in Blantyre every time I did another dreaded ballet exam. The second was because the zoo was virtually next door to the ballet class so I could visit it each week. I was such a regular that I got to help feed some of the animals and go in their enclosures (the safe ones). Seeing Sheba the aged lioness pacing her cage in a zoo in Africa never seemed right to me. I was given my leopard tortoise, and one day, crammed into a closed cardboard box with its clipped wings, Clipper the ground hornbill came home with us. It has to be said she was quite a hideous, ugly bird, jet black with a bright red gullet and a long black beak. However, she did have the most incredibly gorgeously long eyelashes. Clipper and I were inseparable -- until her wing feathers grew back and she flew away. Animals and nature were very much part of everyday life. I had a rescued pigeon living in my bedroom and a python living in the drain outside my bedroom! It was quite obvious from an early age that I was destined to become a vet though really my heart was set on becoming a game warden, like in Born Free, driving around a game park in a battered trusty old Land Rover. Neither of these happened, alas, but I do still have a thing about Land Rovers.

I should explain that from the age of eleven until I was thirteen I boarded a plane six times a year flying 5,000 miles each time to go to school in the UK then home for holidays to see family, Malawi and the animals. With little choice of secondary schools in Malawi, I was sent to Sidcot, a Quaker boarding school near Bristol. Sidcot became my home from home. Phone calls were expensive so letters home, written every Saturday morning, became a lifeline. The post was unreliable and incredibly slow. When I was thirteen I remember receiving a long letter from mum. In it she carefully, bravely, said that she and dad were splitting up and getting a divorce. This was bad enough but at the end she wrote that Hugo, my sheep, had swallowed a plastic bag and died. I was devastated. Everything came crashing down as our parents split up, and much like the caribou and the wildebeest, we left Malawi behind us, distributed all our animals and migrated to Birmingham, UK to live with our dad.

Mum moved to Fife in Scotland. It all took some adjusting, as you can imagine, but eventually we settled and our single dad did a fantastic job. In the holidays we would all hop on a National Express bus destined for Dundee to visit mum. Things were never the same and Africa became just memories.

After leaving Malawi I carried on going to Sidcot. It was a caring school of about 350 pupils displaced from roughly sixty countries for various reasons. School became my family and normal life for me. It was not an impressively academic school however it did nurture and encourage our strengths and talents and I became quite independent. There were moments of boredom and loneliness but I made good friends and I was good at sports. Sidcot had a huge influence on who I am today but I still feel uncomfortable and embarrassed to say I went to a boarding school. I had no choice. When I think of what I did at such a young age... there are children today who have never hopped on a bus and there I was, aged only 11, getting on a bus then a train, then a plane to go home when we lived in Malawi. French was always my weak subject (in fact my worst grade on my report!) so, aged fifteen, in an attempt to improve this, I went on a French exchange for three weeks in the summer holiday. Bearing in mind mobile phones didn't exist, all communication was via letters and a few phone calls between my French family and my dad. My travel arrangements were set and I flew to Paris, took a train to Lyon then changed for a train to Valence where I was to meet my French exchange friend and her father on the platform. I was to wear white dungarees.

I remember feeling very out of my depth and I struggled to find the few French words I thought I knew. Dinner that night was rabbit stew - the rabbits I had been stroking that afternoon! This was going to be difficult. Other culinary experiences were more pleasant, like eating crusty baguettes filled with melting slabs of chocolate and dipping baguette topped with apricot confiture into bowls of hot chocolate for breakfast. The family were lovely, lots of fun and I went to the Alps and to Sête with them. By the end of the three weeks I was coping a bit better with my French and was starting to love being in France. Yes I would definitely come back again. And I did, again and again....

When I left school I was awarded sports person of the year. With the money I bought a mountain bike which I still use today, 39 years later! I also got a travel bursary which, literally, was my ticket to travel. Six months later my brother and I set off to India where we worked as volunteers for ten months. We were based in a small town, Machilipatnam, which was on the coast north of Chennai (formerly Madras) in Andhra Pradesh. Life was simple, basic. We got our water from a well, our milk from buffalos milked daily outside our house and we didn't have a flushing toilet. Rats would scratch the legs of the bed and our only technology was a radio cassette recorder, so we connected to the outside world via the BBC World Service news. It was a very poor town with street stalls, an extravagantly big church and a cinema with one wobbly fan up high. People were gentle, polite and incredibly curious about us. Villagers would come to the roadside to stare and to stroke my long blonde hair when we walked to work – every day for ten months! Sometimes we were invited to a house and given buttermilk to drink – I never did get used to this or grow to like it. People were grateful for anything and this was very humbling. I was a very naïve eighteen year old but I learnt so much. It was challenging but also enjoyable teaching some women to sew and helping children to write letters to their mainly Danish sponsors. India was a fascinating experience and travelling on overcrowded trains and dodgy buses was brilliant and exciting.

I kept a diary which still amuses me. I was interested in people, in cultures and decided I'd quite like to study anthropology one day. I now had the travel bug and I developed a curiosity for adventure. I have definitely inherited my dad's fearless approach to most situations and I have never been afraid of change. At times there were consequences to his fearlessness, often at our expense.

I can remember driving in Hwange game park, Zambia, in our VW Variant with us four children (my little brother crammed into the boot), my parents and my 74 year old Oma (who had come from Holland for a holiday) oh, and lots of luggage, of course. Too busy looking at the warthogs to the right my dad missed the left bend and the car got stuck in some dried elephant footprint craters. *Right kids, you need to get out, take all the luggage off the roof rack and look for some stones to fill the craters.*

This we did without thinking twice and the car was nudged slowly from one crater to the next. All fine except that there was a mother elephant and her calf behind a nearby bush flapping her ears and trumpeting angrily. We carried on calmly, replaced the luggage and continued on our journey. The next stop was for my dad to get out the car and walk closer to get better cine 8 film footage of a rhino.

Once we stayed at Namaso bay on Lake Malawi and my dad took a troop of us kids up a hill where there was a fish eagle's nest up a tree. We climbed up the hill then my dad climbed the tree to get a closer look. Meanwhile the irate fish eagle was squawking and swooshing down trying to gorge my dad's eyes out. This was normal life to us.

Teenage life in Bournville Birmingham ticked along ok. Conflict has never really featured in our upbringing. I can't recall my parents ever fighting or falling out. We weren't a family who argued. Even today I try to avoid conflict or confrontation. We all started to do things with our lives and grew up to be pretty well-balanced, all things considered. We grumbled and begrudgingly carried out our chores around the house. There were disagreements about the chore chart but it was fair to share and we learnt to cook and to fend for ourselves. My dad tended to over-cater so, by the third day, whatever started off became soup, much to our disapproval. It made sense with four children and our single dad trying to make ends meet. We never asked for much or wanted things.

We had many fun times like when dad returned from a trip to India with a special present for us all. He opened his suitcase and produced a large cube. *This is a firework from the Hindu Diwali festival. Let's see what happens shall we?* Fabulous. Excitedly, that night he lit it in our back garden and there was this almighty kaboom! The house shook and the windows rattled like the place was falling down. This amused my dad and us enormously and we were very impressed but....seriously, this firework bomb went on a plane?

Bournville was also a smoke free, noise free, pub free Quaker housing area. Oops!

We went to France for a summer holiday. We had a VW Combi but it was nothing like our Malawi Combi which had lifting up front windows we used to hang out of and, as an ex-ambulance it had a sliding glass partition, a fold up nurse's seat by the back door and a buzzer. My dad converted it into a camper with a stove, a table, beds and mum finished it off with lovely stripy curtains – made, as it happened, out of the same fabric that was used to make the uniforms of the prisoners who did community work around town! We packed our huge tent, packed in all of us and holidayed on a budget driving around rural France. We stole maize and sunflowers from the fields and dad got many bottles of very cheap wine (I think this was his main reason for choosing to go to France!) which we stashed under the seats with strict instructions not to get up as we went through the German customs. All bottles were successfully smuggled in.

Having abandoned my dream of becoming a vet or a game warden I now had to decide what to do with my life. I thought about studying Anthropology but was partly put off by the fact that jobs would be few and far between but also that I would be in situations where I would have to eat unrecognisable foods on my travels. Since I was ten I had already stopped eating lamb in empathy of Hugo my sheep and , when I was sixteen, for animal welfare reasons, I stopped eating meat and became a vegetarian which I still am today, even when it is limited and challenging in France.

I decided to re-take an exam and try my chances at primary teaching. An odd choice as I don't like being on stage or being the centre of attention. For the next four years I studied for a B.Ed(Hons) at Edgehill College in Ormskirk. Typically I only just qualified having been more interested in playing sports and drinking in the bar than buckling down to studying. I got my first job teaching in a primary school in west London. This was difficult being full time with no class assistant and thirty five children in my class, many of whom had very challenging behaviour. But I enjoyed teaching and I think I was quite good at it. My classroom was always highly creative, exciting and fun and I was responsible for art throughout the school. I would look forward to the six week summer holidays when I could travel again. I went to Thailand, Zimbabwe, Fiji, Australia, around Europe, Kenya and Tanzania. Which reminds me about explaining my fear of hyaenas...

It was in Tanzania that I had a near death experience. We set up camp in a very basic camp site high on the edge of the Ngorongoro crater. There were five of us and we found a driver and a cook. I decided to pitch my tent far away from the other couples' tents as I was on my own. My first mistake. We watched the sun set and, after a campfire meal and a few Tanzanian brandies we retreated to our tents. I was snuggled in my sleeping bag ready for a good sleep after a fabulous day, when I could hear the familiar hideous laughing of a pack of hyaenas as they were approaching the campsite to look for scraps around the fires and bins. So this explained why the driver and our cook were sleeping in the van. Closer....closer....closer...louder...louder...louder. I became acutely conscious that there was only a thin membrane of tent fabric separating me from many jaws of these bone crunching, hungry scavengers. I'm sure I stopped breathing. A very bad time to need a wee but this was not an option. I thought that, if they drag me from my tent to eat my bones, no-one would ever know. Many tense moments passed and, thankfully, the sun was rising. All went quiet so I slowly unzipped my tent, checked it was safe then nipped out for a wee. Phew! I went to the other tents to tell them the good news that I was still alive and was met with *What hyaenas?* ... I was not amused!

Back to my journey and it was around this time my stepdad was offered a job in Fiji. After three years he and my mum returned to Scotland where they found it difficult to settle and found the cost of living very expensive. I suggested re-locating to France. Great lifestyle, fantastic weather, my mum spoke good French and it would be more affordable. They packed up and eventually settled in the Dordogne, where they lived a good life for twenty plus years. For us this meant the start of many happy family summer holidays in France. Little did I know this would also become my destiny.

It was 1998 and my personal life was to turn a dramatic corner. I visited a good friend who had moved from being a burnt-out primary teacher in London, up to Bradford to study. She was sharing a house with two women (one being French) and met a boyfriend. On a drunken girls' night out in Leeds, we were in the Courtyard Bar when, coincidentally, so was her boyfriend and his friend Bryan. It was definitely more Bryan's infectious laugh rather than his long pony tail that left an impression on me. We started seeing more of each other which meant many trips up and down the M1 motorway or countless train journeys for me. My then boyfriend and I split up and I bought my first flat in Harrow Wealdstone, London.

It was on my first ski holiday in Andorra that Bryan suggested I came to live with him in Bradford. That was it... I gave in my notice to leave at work, rented out my flat and left London and headed north. I hired a van, rammed all my stuff in it and headed up the M1. Bryan's flat was, let's just say, sparsely furnished with a TV, stereo and two inflatable zebra chairs in the sitting room. Having squeezed my sofa through the front door he wasn't going to get rid of me that easily!

I picked up supply teaching work around Bradford (which was eye-opening) and Bryan worked shopfitting, around the UK. We had lots of fun camping, going to Leeds football matches, socialising, going on annual skiing holidays and then...motorbiking. Bryan took his bike test and got a new Suzuki SV650, bright yellow, of course. I rode pillion until two years later when I took my bike test and bought a lowered BMW 650GS, ice blue. This kick started the next chapter of our lives together.

I confidently and quickly clocked up six hundred miles on my own, beetling all over Yorkshire and the Lake District as we were headed to Spain for a holiday with friends. I remember the excited buzz you get when you board the ferry, wondering where all the other bikers are going. First on, first off we rode to our campsite on the coast not too far from Santander. Bryan and I took off on a day trip to the Picos Europas mountain range, about a three hour ride there. We took the last cable car of the day up to the moonscape pic where Bryan, romantically proposed to me then unromantically we rode back to the campsite through an almighty lightning storm. I had no inkling of the proposal but everyone else did and a party was all set up - assuming I had said yes!

We managed to sell my flat in London and Bryan's flat in Bradford and bought a Victorian house in the woods in the quirky, creative Yorkshire town of Hebden Bridge. Full of interesting artists, musicians and creative free spirits, Hebden was where people could be whoever or whatever they wanted to be. We fitted in well and had many happy years living there. Bryan started drumming again and joined a rock band, gigging locally, for fun. Finally I gave up teaching after I saw a small advert in the window of my favourite, gorgeous florist shop in Hebden, The Willow Garden. Following an amusing interview ending with large glasses of wine, I got the job. Having no real experience of flowers as such I was lucky to work with an incredibly talented team who taught me all I know. It was freezing cold in winter and could get stressful at times but I loved this job and I miss it today.

On 2nd July 2005, we got married in a National Trust barn in Keighley, just down the road. We didn't need or want a gift list but, the day after, a friend and her son brought us a cardboard box. Bryan opened it and there were two tiny, black kittens. She had heard we had a mouse in the house! Shadrack and Floyd became our family. Living in the woods was great for the cats and it was nice to feel away from Hebden but still close. After a while, however, the lack of light, the dampness and the muddy road became more testing. Bryan was working away for weeks at a time and we decided it was maybe time to make some changes. Winter meant ski holidays mainly to the Alps or Andorra but summers always meant family holidays in France with mum in the Dordogne. We went on a motorbike trip to Chamonix, giving us our first taste of riding along spectacularly challenging roads amongst magnificent mountains. We rode 11.6km through the Mont Blanc tunnel, into Italy for lunch! I realised I missed France.

By 2010 we were feeling under pressure for many reasons trying to juggle things in our lives. There must be a better life than this, we thought! So we booked two ferry tickets and set off on our motorbikes. This time we were on a mission: to find where we wanted to live or, at the same time, where we wouldn't want to settle. Now we were excited. After a weekend at the Isle of Wight festival we carried on to Portsmouth and boarded the ferry to St Malo. Riding up the ramp, securing our bikes down, this time it felt different. This wasn't just a holiday. We didn't really have an itinerary or definite plan where we would go; we were just heading south to the Pyrenees. The further south we travelled, the more it rained and rained and rained. We arrived in Pau then headed east, along the Pyrenees to Lourdes -- a dreadful town with hundreds of B&Bs and tacky souvenir shops, loathsome. As skiers we were curious what Cauteret, the ski station, was like. Then we rode up the incredibly steep Tour de France ascent to the Col de Tourmalet. We were in awe of how the cyclists could do this, it was hard enough on a motorbike! We needed a coffee but first we had to move the donkey that was blocking the doorway. The café was a museum paying homage to the Tour de France, a fascinating pit stop and well worth the hill climb. We kept the Pyrenees to our right and continued, still in the rain, through Tarbes and Lannemezan until we reached Foix, in Ariege. It was lunch time and was completely silent but...the rain had stopped at last!

As the sun came out we started to feel more sure of what we were doing here. We were aiming to get to Andorra via Ax-Les-Thermes, a town we knew from when we would stop on the coach transferring from Toulouse to Andorra for skiing. It felt good to be back in Ax and the sun was shining, as it always does in Ax! We took off our helmets, jackets, boots and socks, sat on the edge of the thermal spring and dangled our feet in. We felt at home. How had we forgotten what a lovely town Ax was? Surrounded by mountains we felt re-energised.

By the time we reached Andorra our motorbike jackets were steaming in the warm sunshine. We loved the nifty switchback roads and the incredible views around every bend. This was what we were looking for. We stayed overnight then rode towards Spain. We had to stop as this cute little yellow train trundled passed us chugging up the mountain. We said that one day we hoped we would ride on that train.

We descended through endless vineyards, the warm sunshine becoming scorching hot as we approached Perpignan. We carried on to Narbonne where we rested for a couple of nights. It was lovely but far too flat! After ambling around the market and eating a few ice creams we rode on to Carcassonne, a UNESCO heritage site. Wow, the spectacular, fairytale castle set against the back drop of a blue sky was breathtaking. We found a great little place to stay where we could wallow in our own plunge pool while looking out at La Cité, even more majestic lit up at night. We loved it around here. Our grand tour ended with a short stop at mum's in the Dordogne on the way to St Malo and back to the UK.

Hebden didn't feel like home any more just an anti-climax. Strangely, a clairvoyant was in town so a few of us thought it would be interesting to see what she had to say. Never being convinced about things like this I was, however, quite curious. What harm could it do? I took off my wedding ring and adopted an expressionless face, giving away no clues. Sitting in this scruffy room with nothing but a table and a pack of cards was this old lady. She started turning cards then paused, revealing a card that had a picture of a ship and a cage on it. *Interesting,* she said. *You are feeling trapped and will be going on a journey, maybe across water, where you will feel free.* She was spot on and that was it. I knew I was never meant to stay in the UK so France, here we come...

Action plans began. We rented out our house in Hebden, got the cats their passports to travel and, with regret, we sold both our motorbikes, intending to replace them in France (less complicated than registering them, we thought). We had a leaving party with French food and red, white and blue bunting.

On 11th April 2011 we packed the van and my car with our things, and the cats. Not knowing what I could do to earn a living, I packed soap-making and floristry equipment thinking I could have a market stall. Feeling excited, relieved and slightly apprehensive, finally we were beginning our journey across the channel. We dropped off the cats at my mum's as we had arranged with a family who lived in La Bastide de Serou, near St Girons,

Ariege to stay with them and in return we worked on their barn roof and garden. Our first experience of living in France was great and we made good friends, worked hard, the roof was finished and the garden improved. It rained far too much and the green scenery just wasn't dramatic enough. This wasn't where we would live.

Then I found a house to rent in Mercus Gabaret, about ten minutes south of Foix. I collected the cats and we all lived happily and peacefully in this ancient stone house with its lovely garden perched at the top of the village. It was basic but it suited us. I saw a seasonal job advertised in Ax, had an interview and got the job working in an outdoor shop selling high-end skiing, walking, climbing and other outdoor equipment which was packaged, by me, in the atelier, and sent all over the world. I worked in a team with French, English, Italian, Russian and Basque colleagues. It was very tiring at first but, slowly, I gained confidence and my French started to improve. It made me realise how basic my French really was but everyone was very patient and good humoured especially when I would mispronounce something I wanted to say and it meant something completely different, usually rude. Once I thought I was saying that I liked the design on a pair of skis I was packing when, actually what I had said was that I liked the titty tassels! Endless amusement for all! The perk of the job was that I got a free lift pass to ski all season which was fabulous. It took a while to get used to downing tools at midday and going off for a two hour lunch break. It had been a long time since I had had a proper one of those.

Over the next three years we moved a few times. We rented an old discotheque in Orgeix, with a slightly deranged land lady. We escaped from there and rented a skinny three storey old stone house at the top of a very small mountain village, Ascou, about ten minutes up a twisty road from Ax. It was unfurnished which literally meant it had a shower, a small table and a wood burning stove. I got a mattress and we slept on the floor. I borrowed a fridge after a few weeks, a camping stove and ten months later (after dreaming of lasagne, baked potatoes and cakes) a kind neighbour lent me an oven which was wheeled down the road and installed with much laughter. Life was simple but good. The house had two carved wood balconies where we would sit at night with a glass of vin rouge watching the bright lights of the piste bashers (*dameurs*) ploughing and levelling the pistes ready for the next day's skiing across the valley in Les Trois Domaines ski station. I had no spare money, no tv, no wifi and limited phone use for a year, so I used my time being creative or reading.

One of the things I loved most about living in the Pyrenees was how dramatic the seasons were. Winter was challenging and I soon realised I was not very well prepared. The snow fell thick and fast with long icicles dangling off the guttering. The snow was so deep outside the front door I had to dig a waist-high trench out to the road. I had to park the car at the bottom of the village as the road was like an ice slide for a few weeks. There were many days when I would put on my snow boots to walk down to my car which I couldn't see as snow had completely covered it. I would clear enough snow to open the door then start the engine and heater and finish clearing the car and digging a channel so I could drive out, all using my plastic chopping board! Annoyingly, by the time I drove back from work someone would have nipped into my space so I'd have to dig again....

I felt fit from carrying supplies up through the village and I learnt to be more organised, especially when Bryan was away working and I was on my own. The wood burner was my only heat and I quickly ran out of wood but couldn't get more delivered until the snow had melted. It was cold, so cold that I would warm a couple of stones on the wood burner then put them in the bed to warm it. The cats and I cuddled together to share our warmth. My neighbours were friendly, kind but it was difficult communicating with my basic French. I did my best.

When I did get wifi connected I opened an online ETSY shop called Atelier Mooch and I started to sell things I found in local *brocantes* and *vide greniers* (French equivalent to junk shops and car boot sales but so much nicer and more interesting). Collecting became my passion and I would look forward to Sundays. The spare room started to fill up! I did well with my shop and it justified my love of collecting nice things. I never get bored, I'm good at occupying myself and I don't mind my own company. It had been three years now and Bryan and I decided now was a good time to sell our house in Hebden, to cut ties with the UK, to take the plunge -- to migrate properly to France.

There was no more seasonal work for me so I moved to be with my mum in the Dordogne and put all my energy into house hunting. We couldn't afford to buy in or near Ax so my search got wider and it covered a vast area. Armed with post-it notes and red, green and yellow pens, a map and a tent I drove all over, exploring. What we wanted and what we could afford became a challenge. A garden, garage and outbuildings were top of our list as well as being walking distance to a bar and *boulangerie*. Ideally we wanted a house we could make money from as a gite or B&B. I viewed thirty-eight properties from the Montagnes Noir north of Carcassonne, to Mirepoix, to Limoux. I drove and drove to see places you would never otherwise go to. A great way to orientate yourself, but tiring. Most viewings were in French but I could cope now and I learnt new, useful house buying words.

Eventually I drove through Limoux and headed south to a town called Quillan. A work colleague in Ax had mentioned Quillan saying it was a great, lively town. He often visited a friend who lived there. It was only 53km from Ax and a stunningly beautiful journey but we never went there, why? I pitched my tent in the municipal campsite on a hill with amazing views of the Trois Quilles mountain peaks. This felt special. I ventured into town. There was a charming rustic scruffiness about the buildings and a great sense of history - an époque of grander times. But where were all the people? It seemed so quiet. I spent a few weeks in the campsite and Quillan really grew on me. I loved how it is a nest amongst the mountains, crags and peaks, the river Aude meandering through the town, under the old bridge and the austere ancient fort dominating the town and overlooking the patchwork of terracotta roof tiles. It is picturesque but unpretentious, a town with real people, families, tourists , settlers and drifters.

Quillan is an easy town to live in with everything at your fingertips. Market days bring the community together while people natter as they stock up on what they need or fancy. Seeing all the incredible edibles temptingly displayed, the smells of fresh fruit, the misshaped homegrown vegetables, the different grades of goats cheeses, tempting piles of olives, a range of clothing for sale, from old French housewife tabards (house coats) to pairs of *pantouffles* (what a great word for a pair of slippers!). The French really do love their *pantouffles*. The bars are buzzing with customers meeting for coffees or an early beer. Quillan is a lively town that rarely really sleeps. There is never a dull day. Quillan can be whatever you want it to be. Residents are dynamic and diverse, colourful and quirky, fit or unfit. How people find this little town at the far end of the Pyrenees will always intrigue me. Those of us who are not native to Quillan have much in common, a good starting place for great friendships. We are here because either we feel we don't belong somewhere else or maybe it's because we have been lured to France by what we love to do, be it skiing, running, walking, photography, art, you name it. We have all migrated and drifted here from all over the world. We all have a story to tell, some choose not to. We are all following our dreams, living our dreams but are not all dreamers. A few leave but more arrive and stay. Some are lucky enough to be retired but others still have to eek a living doing what others need them to do.

Phew, finally we had found a place where we wanted to live. Next we found a house. It was in the main square, Place de la République, and didn't need too much work so we could move in straight away. It didn't have a garden or outbuildings but it was a couple of minutes from four bars! We offered, signed and six months later we moved in. Our roof had been vandalised and was in a shocking state. Consequently we had to deal with three months of leaks and flooding until the roof was replaced. This created lots of commotion in the square and we got to meet many people very quickly. We were astonished at how many English speakers lived in Quillan, we really had no idea. The local French residents seemed to be very tolerant and accepting of the foreigners in town, much to our surprise. No.5 became our first owned house in France.

Living in the main square, the hub of Quillan, had its challenges. It was great watching the summer entertainment sitting on our balcony, our royal box. We really had no idea of the scale of the entertainment and the volume of the noise and happenings that were to come over the summer months. I needed an escape so we found a large garden plot to rent, a short walk from our house. This became my sanctuary, my peaceful space and I was delighted and happy clearing, digging, planting, harvesting and re-connecting with nature. There were big grasshoppers, quick lizards, small blackish scorpions, spotted hoopoes and a few snakes which were usually basking against the stone wall while it heated up - evoking memories of my childhood in Africa. I would leave my watch and phone at home and I would lose track of time, totally absorbed in happy business.

We worked hard creating two en-suite bedrooms and opened a B&B. This was very successful and we had many bookings. At first, having strangers in the house took some getting used to but we enjoyed meeting our guests and some even moved to Quillan and have become very good friends. A combination of my obsessive restlessness and having a head with far too many ideas floating about I knocked down the corridor wall on the ground floor while Bryan was working away (I did get advice first!) and decided the space would make a great *salon de thé*. That was it, I started hoarding my ideas and felt excited about what it could look like. Bryan worked tirelessly trying to satisfy my crazy ideas. I practised cake baking and perfecting my scones. I sourced tasty teas and was in my element tweaking the décor. I had found a place for lots of my *brocante* finds, at last. Le Petit Monde (the small world) finally opened its doors and we felt really proud. It was very popular. My scones and cakes sold out and everyone was so supportive, enthusiastic and we felt very encouraged. Quillan needed this and it was working. But I had underestimated just how much hard work it would be baking three times a week for hours, shopping for supplies, taking orders, serving, washing up, cleaning, everything on my own. One thing that was great was that my French started to improve chatting to our local customers.

I was just getting into a rhythm with running Le Petit Monde and Bryan had already stopped working away in the UK when, after seven intense months the Covid-19 pandemic struck and we were forced to close. Such a shame. It did give us some time to think things over and, post-pandemic, we decided to try to sell our house and look for a peaceful house with a garden, still in Quillan. Thinking it could take a year we were shocked and astounded when we sold in three days! We found another house which has a huge garden and the only noises are the croaky frogs and the hooting owls; no more rugby singing, no more drunks to deal with and, best of all , no one knows if we are at home. In the mornings I am happiest when I am pottering eccentrically in my greenhouse in my pyjamas with a mug of tea! We both ride motorbikes again and belong to a growing motorbike group of great friends. Bryan hasn't really picked up his drum sticks but there's plenty of time for that. We lost Floyd but still have Shadrack who is now a fat, black eighteen year old cat who loves his new big garden – a far cry from his days hanging around the bars in the square.

Our back garden looks out to the mountain peaks that surround Quillan and I will never tire of this view that changes so dramatically with the seasons. I love that, whenever I feel like it, I can shut the front gate and go out exploring, walking or running along the wild trails or cycle along deserted, often challenging roads where I soak up the solitude, the peace and quiet with breath-taking scenery and surrounded by nature. I hear woodpeckers tapping, *chasse* (hunting) dogs frantically barking, the crescendo of cicadas and leaves rustling when a deer disappears. My senses have woken up here but most of all I love the silence and being close to nature again. Who could ask for more?

I still dream of one day living in a rustic, rickety stone farmhouse in the foothills of the Pyrenees surrounded by collected and rescued animals, with land to dig and grow and maybe a rusty trusty Land Rover parked up. I believe things happen for a reason and that this is our destiny, our fate. Do we have any regrets moving to France? Yes, one and it is not moving out here many years before we did. We go back to the UK less and less, we miss it less and less and we are happy to be here.

La vie est belle.

We still have work to do before we open another B&B which will be called Le Perchoir. Translated this means a perch or roost, like coming home to roost. The thinking behind this is that each summer the sky above Quillan is filled with swallows, house martins and swifts diving to catch the evening insects and who have all skilfully, incredibly, migrated back to Quillan to roost in last year's nest to rear the next generation of chicks. For some this is just the beginning, for others it marks the end of a very long journey. Is this the end of my journey? My migration? Who knows, I like change so I'm not sure ....

Michelle's Story

I'm going to write about my journey to France. I mean my actual journey from Cheshire to the South of France. It's not that straightforward.

My journey started with me, a six year old boy and a Peugeot 206 packed with what I thought I might need. There was no real plan as such, just a random woman in a small village in France who offered me a rented house with what she described as a perfect opportunity to embrace the French life. It turned out to be not what it seemed. The accommodation was over-priced and to make up the monthly rent I would be expected to look after her son, her dogs and to be on hand for any other jobs she required me to do. I was essentially treated like one of her many volunteers. These are the unpaid skivvies that help these people to live their dreams.

I was forty-nine years old with a six year old son, not some carefree whipper-snapper from Australia that just wanted an adventure. Please don't judge me, I had discussed this at length with my husband. We'd always dreamed of living in France when our two boys had flown the nest. We'd just had a few obstacles in the way. Another child came along unexpectedly in our 40s, I had a long illness, then heart surgery, the usual stuff.

We did discuss it at length over a couple of bottles of wine on our usual Saturday date night.

We've been doing date night for over thirty years. We invented it!

He said: *There is no reason why you and Gabriel can't go.*
I said: *OK.*
He said: *I will still work here and come at weekends.*
I said: *OK.*
He said: *OK.*

The journey to Portsmouth was interesting. I'd never been there and we didn't have Sat Nav in those days. It was a Sunday so traffic was sparse but that is also when the highway people decide it's a good opportunity to fix the motorways. There were diversions all over the show. However, we made it on time for the ferry. Just.

We landed in Santander the next day. My hand written map inexplicably guided us onto the correct route. What I remember of that eleven hour journey was, it was long, Gabriel was a star, dropping coins in the kiosk on the *péage.* We did a bit of a detour around Biarritz, I battled the lanes in Toulouse in rush hour traffic. I did finally make it to the outskirts of Quillan at 11:00pm. Exhausted, I managed to contact my husband, I couldn't find the village. He contacted my host and she kindly checked us in to a hotel in Quillan for the night.

So this is when the story really starts. 31st August 2011, the first week I arrived, I had to get my son into school. My host gave me a letter that I took to the *Maire* saying whatever it said. I will never fully understand whether or not she was just taking the piss but the look on the faces of these people made me feel like I had just entered a competition for world class chess when I was a champion of tiddlywinks. Joking apart, I got him into school that week and he thrived...

He said: *Mummy, this is the worst day of my life...* every day for eight months.
He said: *I hate you.*
He said: *I want to go back to England.*
He said: *I can't speak French.*
He said: *I can't speak to you.*
He said: *I hate you more.*

He did eventually speak at school, he later told me he was terrified of getting things wrong so he wouldn't speak.

There was a lovely moment once when the phone rang and he answered it. He then handed me the phone, very excited, saying *Mummy, the Queen's on the phone.* Now this doesn't necessarily translate in written form but the person on the phone said *Bonjour Madame, c'est Lorraine.* If you understand French this can be heard as *La Reine*. God love him, he was convinced.

I threw myself into my life in France. I live in a very small village, close to Quillan. I went to every event that involved alcohol, music and anything remotely to do with children. Luckily for me, my neighbours were French, old and intrigued. Why on earth would a, seemingly, normal woman come to live here from the UK? It was a hoot. I genuinely love old people, they have stories, memories, patience, they were young once. We were accepted with open arms even when my husband told the neighbour that we ate a stray dog (he couldn't work out how to say we fed the stray dog). The language will always be tricky but we get along just fine.

So how did we make it work? Money helps. My husband did commute for a few years but circumstances changed and a healthy redundancy package enabled us to renovate our old village house and left enough for us to live for a few years. How do you survive in France without a job or a pension. We both had final salary pensions to look forward to but were a few years off sixty. We needed to think of something creative. My husband is a talented cook so we started to think about how we could somehow make a living from this talent.

The idea came to us quite quickly. Indian food wasn't something that was readily available in this part of France. There was a large English speaking community that we knew missed their curry fix. We started on markets in 2017. We built up a good customer base, however, it was tough. We couldn't anticipate how much curry to make. Sometimes we came home with loads (if the weather was bad). There is only so much curry our son could stomach. So my husband created a menu as close to an Indian Takeaway as possible. We were going to be the first Indian Food delivery service in rural France, I think that is true. We would deliver once a week, on a Friday, to locations around the area. What helped massively for us was that we went into lockdown a few months after we started. We were encouraged to carry on by the government because we were obviously helping the economy. People couldn't go out to eat so they stayed in with a curry. I can honestly say we were exhausted. We were delivering to locations around the Aude and Ariège. We had to deal with the Gendarmes who didn't really understand the concept, some were pretty scary, some were completely amazing. Most weeks we were making in excess of a hundred curries plus rice, naan breads and starters etc... It was hugely successful and continues to be although we're glad we don't get as many orders nowadays.

We are trying to slow down now and enjoy our life in France a bit more leisurely. Our pensions have eased our financial situation and our youngest son will be 18 this year. I don't stress about doing everything French now. I have English speaking friends, I've joined an English speaking drama group who put on amazing pantomimes every year. Apparently I'm not bad, I got the leading lady part the second time I was involved (that might be an indication of how bad it is) but I kid you not, it's bloody brilliant.

I have learnt not to say a bad word about Johnny Hallyday, to understand the *chasse* (the local hunt) and never underestimate the need to have an English speaking hairdresser. So it's time for us to do a bit of travelling, methinks.

So, that's it. We did it. We invented date nights and we invented Indian Takeaway in rural France. *Bonne Chance.*

Nicky's Story

A Bright Irreverent Nutcase

I think the voice of convention says to women: *get married, have a family, a career and above all stay thin.* I missed out the first two, I got the third and as for being thin well that's a bloody minefield of self-loathing that divides women whilst they are manipulated and exploited by the massively lucrative diet industry. Corporate nastiness features a lot in my story. *Baguettes and Blanquette* is a meaningful title to me with great relevance to women. Indulge in carbs and booze I say, with gusto my dears.

Unconventional women are featured throughout this book and I believe that is a strong connection we have to one another. Unique, off-beat, individualistic women coming together in a very unique place, a very beautiful, relatively unknown valley in France. If you strive too hard to get everything that it seems everyone else has or that you are conditioned to think you should have, you can miss out on the unknown, the unexpected and the truly wonderful.

All through my twenties I was in a crazy up and down relationship. But despite being totally incompatible, miraculously, we parted not as friends but not as enemies either. I am grateful we came to an understanding because he died less than a year after we split up. I met the love of my life Jim three months before he died. We had time to fall in love before the storm of his untimely death hit us.

I was told he went to sleep in a backpacker hostel, having uncharacteristically left a bar in Sydney earlier than his friends. He said he was tired. He never woke up again …ever.

The funeral was big. The church was full. I was there with my dad. All of our friends were with his family. At first his family asked me not to come, then they relented. They had extreme grief to deal with and of course I understood that. I think I was an embarrassment. Or maybe it was just the fact that I didn't love him like they did. Young dead people and people recovering from brain surgery are not perfect people, they are just bloody unlucky. To some I was to blame for his death, they needed someone to blame. I had to embrace notoriety. I was gossiped about and vilified by some, though many were extremely kind. Life and in this case death pushes you in a direction. I was in love by then with Jim. *Lean on me,* he said and I did. Everyone forgave everyone in the end. It's very important to live a life you want. Some people are taken so young. He was only thirty-three.

I was full of anguish for quite a long time, possibly three years. I find three years is a time span for many things. It takes a year to understand or learn something, then a year being or doing it and then a year letting it go.

When I was forty-three after several very happy years with Jim and the kids I had a huge set back. I had a miscarriage and it took about three years to get over it.

It's just part of my life now but it was the very worst thing that ever happened to me. It was profoundly sad and I am thankful to Jo and the other storytellers for the opportunity to be able to write about it. I want to mention it because this book is about women. I want to say out loud that miscarriage is not something to be silent about. I just couldn't talk about it for a very long time. I still can't watch scenes in films that include baby loss. I don't need sympathy. I just want to make it clear that miscarriage is a terrible terrible thing. Life shapes you though doesn't it and everything pushes you in a direction.

I felt that I hadn't had much of what I wanted from life or things hadn't happened for me like I thought they would so I was damn well going to find a way to be happy and live a life to suit me. I thought if I worked really hard I would be rewarded – that was before I realised what an awful bunch of sleazy horrid people there are in the business world. There are plenty of great inspirational people of course. Every time I say something negative I feel I must immediately acknowledge the positive, its like I must present a balanced view at all times. I think I'm the bloody BBC. Well actually they aren't balanced anymore are they but let's not get controversial. It's the truly awful people that stick out though; there were a lot of them but more about that later. I'd really like this book to be published so I can't name names – but Traitor Trev (not your real name) I hope you are reading this, you total piece of slimy shit.

Jim and I hatched a plan for a happy life together in France. Retiring together when he was fifty-four and I was just fifty. We decided to get on with making it happen. For a couple of working class kids like us it was a very big dream, but we did it, we are doing it and we are extremely proud of ourselves. We are here living this life not on a whim. We had a goal and we lived our lives always with our goal in mind. There were a few other things that needed to happen of course, we needed Jim's kids to grow up for one, but we were pretty sure they would visit us in the sunshine, which they do and with grandkids now too.

We would need an income in France and enough money to live on without too much work. We decided we needed to rent out our properties in the UK so that we would always have an income in France. Jim had already enabled me to realise my long held dream to go to university. He had his own business and I moved in with him and his boys and went off to Oxford Brookes. It was a magical time for us. Of course I wanted his dream of living abroad one day to come true as well. I felt I needed a Law degree so that I could earn much more money. I studied hard and I loved every moment of being a mature student.

I had to swear an oath to be able to use the famous Oxford Bodleian library. Brookes and Oxford Uni share some things but the Bodleian law section is housed in an ugly 70's block out of town, near a very beautiful park. There are huge legal tomes that have to be digested in order to get an LLB. My dad still does sometimes (and my gran used to) put LLB on my birthday cards. Miss Nicola Holifield LLB. It's Latin, *Legum Baccalaureus.* It means Batchelor of Laws. Batchelor eh? That seems a bit sexist to me but maybe changing it is a bit like taking down statues. In a world that seems to go backwards in so many ways their existence reminds us that the past is often not better than now.

Legal books cost a fortune to buy and go out of date quickly but Oxford Brookes and Oxford Uni students alike all go to the library and Blackwell's to read *Nutshells and Nutcases.* They are brightly bound irreverent little books that simplify everything. *A bright irreverent nutcase*, I'd like that to describe me.

University was a way to prove that I was as good as everyone else. The fear of being judged as inferior in some way runs deep for me. I have never believed I am inferior. It's being judged that bothers me. I despise judgmental people. Is it a female thing or an English thing? Sexism albeit pushed under-ground is alive and kicking but more than that I think it's the divisions in English society that affected me. I've encountered a lot of snobbery in my life. People never use that word anymore do they, but snobs exist, if your accent or your address, your car and clothes aren't quite fitting. I think it's a travesty that the gap between rich and poor gets ever wider in the UK.

I also believe that lack of confidence holds so many women back. I was too shy to ask for any help. I studied on my own. I went to lectures and seminars but I didn't get more than twenty minutes personal tuition in three years. It was readily available. I just felt too old, silly, not posh enough. I got a 2:1 though and I got a first for my dissertation. It was called *Wednesdbury Unreasonableness – the final curtain?* It compared the English law principle of unreasonableness with the European concept of proportionality and declared the latter the future. Bloody Oxford Uni boy Brexit Boris and his cronies undermined not only my life in France but also my dissertation. We made it though so *Up yours Boris.*

I loved Constitutional and European law. At Brookes we came to the strong conclusion led by our professor that it was not legally possible for the UK to leave the EU. I wish we had not drawn that conclusion. I may have moved to France sooner had I known what was to come. Brexit was a terrible blow but I give thanks to the Universe that I was already living in France when it happened. On that day in June 2016 I felt very sad but overwhelmingly relieved. If we had left it later or decided to just work a couple more years, the loss of European rights might have made us too scared to move.

My graduation party was one of the happiest days of my life. Everyone I loved was there and I paid extra to flounce around in the cap and gown all day. It was very special to walk up on the stage to receive my degree to cheers from my family and friends.

I got my Law Degree when I was thirty-six. I was really too old to get on the legal career ladder but luckily I thought I was still young. Perception is everything and I had a lucrative career in procurement for fourteen years. I wanted to earn lots of money. My logic was that I didn't really like working, so if I had to work then I wanted to get paid lots. So I worked extremely hard during those years. Eventually I was part of the Procurement senior leadership team of a big company. I had a team of seven at one point. I was a great boss and I had a really great boss too. He taught me to be confident. That and my Law degree really helped me. Not my knowledge of law that came in handy, no, my inner knowledge that I had a degree that was the self-esteem boosting element. Women need to be confident. You can be nice at the same time, but give confidence a shot. That's my advice.

I tried to be sensible with the money, after all I was working for my new life in France but when you have hardly any life outside of work sometimes you spend money in very stupid ways. Some things are necessary like a cleaner. If you have a busy life and can afford it, don't feel guilty, get a cleaner and live life. Silly restaurants aren't worth the money and Gucci shoes in the airport on the way to a work thing, well I didn't need to do that. I loved those shoes though and they lasted about three years. Lots of things last three years; shoes, grief, jobs, University. Anyhow, sometimes you have no time to choose or consider things properly but I always had our goal in mind. I tried to relish my family and friends since I knew one day I would be too far away to pop by for a cup of tea. I do have quality time with my family, I visit lots and they visit me but I miss them so much it hurts my heart sometimes.

My small business in France has taught me the value of being self-employed and if I have one regret in life it is that I didn't learn this fact sooner. I sell second-hand clothing at big, noisy, boozy gatherings in my house. It's very popular, makes a little bit of money and has connected lots of women. *Vinted* is hard to compete against though, so big business is again the bane of my life. When you work like crazy for a big salary it is hard to connect your time to your money, it just seems remote. You are grateful to and dependent on somebody thinking you are good enough to get a big salary. So you have to prove yourself over and over again every day. When you work for yourself the money you make is your own creation. It's such a great feeling, so different to getting a salary. *Adore Encore* makes a tiny fraction of my old salary but I'm proud of it.

Anyhow why did I give up my big salary job when I was only fifty to live in rural France? Well I couldn't wait. In fact those that doubted me, thought I *was* my job. I wasn't. I did want to prove my worth but my career was always just a means to an end. I wanted to make some money and then give up working. I went to sleep most nights thinking about work. I woke up every morning – planning my day at work. I did not properly rest at the weekend. I got very upset on Sunday afternoons, especially if I'd escaped for a long weekend. My alarm went off at 6, I often worked till 9 pm and sometimes much later. I always had my life in France as my goal, otherwise I could not have been so committed to my corporate life.

The pressure did not come entirely from my boss and our targets. It was also internal pressure. I was very self-motivated. I wanted to be the best and I did beat everyone else consistently. My team always over achieved our target. We were undoubtedly the best procurement team in history. I tried hard to be happy. I was always laughing, smiling, telling the team we had to enjoy work but for the most part I absolutely hated it.

Now here comes Mrs BBC, Angela Rippon because she has long legs like me. It's a joke actually my legs are not long, just longish for a short person that's all. There were some fantastic achievements, I was proud, there was loads of fun, and I had trappings. I had freedom. I worked at home a lot. I worked with some brilliant people over the years. However there were some truly truly awful people and I'm going to enjoy writing about how revolting they are in the hope they might or others might recognise who they are. I would like to thank each one of them from the bottom of my heart; they galvanised me, they hastened me and they changed my life.

Let's start with Traitor Trev. I really thought he was my friend. I was very unhappy with the way I had been treated by some other revolting people, so I was trying to get another job and obviously I didn't want my boss to know. I confided in Trev that I had applied for a job outside the company. He told my boss my intentions the very same day. He had nothing to gain, he was just an arse-licking bastard with a badly fitting suit and bald head and he betrayed me. That doesn't sound particularly terrible I know but it was the deep sincerity he conveyed to me and then the incredible speed at which he betrayed me. I think it was probably less than ten minutes. He definitely wasn't the worst. Small fry you are Trev, a tiny little tiddler of a man. I despised you then, now you are relegated to an amusing story.

The worst was not the Big Cheese either. With two grovelling acolytes at his side like Gripper and his mates in *Grange Hill*, he accused me of calling him a bully to his team. The irony was lost on everyone present except me. I was bullied by them and particularly so in that meeting but I stood my ground and said *Yes Big Cheese indeed you are a bully.* A week later in the team meeting, in front of about thirty people without telling me in advance, he announced two people were being parachuted in to save my projects, Traitor Trev and Octavia. The implication was of course that I had failed to deliver. I definitely had not. Years later I re-examined my work dispassionately with objectivity and it was very good. I had failed to communicate progress properly or ask for help, that's all. I was brought up not to show off. Jim said Trev and Octavia would get their parachutes stuck in a tree. That image stayed with me and it really helped lessen the humiliation.

Thirty pairs of eyes looking at me with sympathy and curiosity and relief it wasn't them being picked on. It's seventeen years ago and it still makes me quiver and feel nauseous thinking about it. I was on the verge of walking out there and then. I nearly did. I wish I had. It would be a better story. I masochistically stayed nearly another year and tried to repair my reputation and prove everyone wrong. I have learnt now that if someone wants to think badly of you just let him or her, don't waste too much energy. There are other people out there who won't think that. However, because in Jim's words I had gone from *Hero to Zero* very quickly, I responded by working ever harder to prove the bullies all wrong.

I know now without a shadow of a doubt that Trev and Octavia did not have my skills. I knew it then too really but Big Cheese just got things so badly wrong and his nasty acolytes agreed with everything he said. A particularly duplicitous one called Clive turned against Big Cheese too in the end I believe. Although he shouted and swore a lot Big Cheese had a good reputation. For the most part he did have good judgment and he was skilled, but he was completely wrong about me and there was something else he got really wrong too. He was anonymously character assassinated and lots of personal details and criticism were sent to the board. He thought it was his secretary. Evidently he was pretty broken by the accusations. He rang everyone personally about it. All bullies are extremely sensitive. It was not his secretary. It was the quiet guy in the corner that everybody liked. If I know this secret then so do lots of other people but nobody as far as I know ever told him. A few years later when I had my own team I would not have employed either Trev or Octavia even for very junior roles but I might have given Big Cheese a trial.

I forgive you, all the shallow shell people without decency that I worked with. It's not your fault, it's the terrible pressure and the consumerism and the traffic going to work every day that stresses you out and the complete exhaustion that turns you into corporate horrors. *Smelly cat it's not your fault, it's what they are feeding you.* Phoebe Buffay.

Octavia was a short-term contractor on a huge rate of £800 per day, oodles more than me. Big Cheese made her my boss, that meant me sharing everything I'd worked hard on with her and her belittling me. I'd been working myself to exhaustion. I just needed a bit of a steer, someone to listen to my ideas, help me with connections, share experience, guide me. I was aloof because I was working so hard and just like University, I never ever asked for help. I was still under the assumption that my own department had my back. I was so sweetly innocent then. They didn't.

Octavia asked me to do extremely menial things for her like cut and pasting her documents, the absolute cheek of it. She unilaterally cancelled my meetings which damaged my reputation and undermined my authority. She presented my work as her own, just reformatted a bit. She rang her husband for advice on projects. She shared confidential information with him. He mixed in very senior business circles. He bought her a Jag, she flicked her blond hair about, told me she modelled whilst at University and casually destroyed the essence of me. Many months later they realised she was totally out of her depth and Big Cheese and another guy of his ilk took her into a room and I suspect destroyed her too. She immediately left the building in tears, never to return. She was a victim too. I never heard from her again. She disappeared from the job market entirely as far as I could tell.

One day I had said: *I will not work with Octavia for one more moment, so I resign with immediate effect.* Oh the drama! Big Cheese didn't accept my resignation, instead he moved me to work for two people, so effectively two jobs. He gave me three projects that everyone else, including Traitor Trev, had failed to deliver. I think there was probably a recruitment ban. He was scared of another potential tribunal issue. I heard there were several ongoing against him. He told me he was very disappointed in me. I really wish I'd told him to fuck off. I suppose I can do it now. *Fuck off you twat face bully prick.* Him refusing my resignation was absolutely nothing to do with me at all, but oh joy I had another chance to work myself to death.

I smashed all the silly projects. I succeeded in repairing my reputation and I left just as the whole department was having a huge crisis that hit the newspapers and involved a Government minister. It was a double spread in a broadsheet in 2010 and the headline was *Company X's Big Bad Wobble*. I kept the article for a while. I wish I still had it. I could put it in a frame and hang it in the downstairs loo. They asked me to come and help them at the weekend because of the scandal, they even asked me to stay on a couple of months. I said no. Well I said: *Pay me as much as Octavia and I will.* They said no of course. I think Big Cheese eventually realised he had misjudged me. I nearly left very soon after the parachute thing but for a while I was glad I hadn't because not much later I found out I was pregnant, but you already know how that turned out. I would not have coped with any of it – if we didn't have our escape to France plan. I was working for our dream.

I went back to my previous employer and it was for the most part an extremely rewarding job. My boss was an inspiration and support but there was still lots of drama, blood on the board room floor. But I had hardened up and I trusted my boss which made everything okay and I tried hard to make sure my team were never treated like I was. I was successful to a point, except for Foxy Bingo, the most horrid man I ever had the displeasure to meet. He did everything he could to undermine me. He was vile to my team and me. He instructed his people to withhold information. He was a director and I wasn't. He had more power than me. He tried very hard to discredit my work. That work involved a great deal of blood, sweat and tears. He had clout and the board listened to him. I proved my deals were best for the business over and over and over again. I really cared about what was best for the company, a fact which amazes me now because it is so obvious that they did not care a jot about me. Why on earth would they? I was so naïve, though My deals were in fact exemplary and were independently judged as such much later by incredibly expensive consultants. I worked for months late into the evening to prove Foxy Bingo wrong. He disliked me because I was in charge of the procurement of travel and temporary labour and he wanted to deliver it with his huge team of people in Liverpool and he also liked to travel first class and stay in posh hotels with his boyfriend on Friday nights. The only problem was that he was utterly useless and out of date, just like his brown tweed three-piece suit. I was all about the logic and doing my job.

I see now, through writing this story, that he probably had good reasons and wanted to save jobs. I was just collateral damage. I'm so annoyed that I'm so very understanding now. I have found perspective with the glow of living in France all around me and with the benefit of hindsight it turns out that the people weren't the horrors at all, not even the worst one of all, Foxy Bingo. It was corporate life that is horrible. Exciting though it is at times. I had some fantastic moments, but I don't miss it. I appreciate every day I escaped the rat race. It truly is absolute rats racing to the top, no matter what.

A well-paid job was always a means to an end for me. I felt from a young age that surely there was more to life than being born, working till age sixty-five with four or five weeks off a year. Surely that was not *it*. I didn't know what I wanted. I just knew that I didn't want that.

It turns out there are quite a few people who feel just the same, with all sorts of stories and dreams and there is a huge magnet that has drawn some of them to this tiny little bit of France. Thanks very much Traitor Trev, Big Cheese and Foxy Bingo for your input into my life and Project France. You were truly the wind below the Ryanair wings that took me to my new life, you great big puffs of smoke and wind.

Thank you so much. I rest the heel of my adopted French hand under my chin and swipe my hand with force upwards to you.

Melissa's Story

The draw to Quillan

I set off from Narbonne and drive south. I don't know where I'm going, just a pin in the map; Antugnac. But first I have to go to Quillan to meet the estate agent. The drive is long and more of rural France unfolds before me. The scenery is starting to change, I'm leaving behind the hay bales and flat openness, the mountains are looming in the distance. I feel different, there is something calling me. My heart knows where it's going, my head stays in its usual state of trying to keep up. The grape vines are saying this way. I follow signs for Carcassone and then Limoux. The road to Limoux is lined by what I call army trees with their camouflaged trunks directing my path: should I falter they will correct me or kill me.

I pass through more small towns, Esperaza, Campagne and many saint's names. All the time the river runs along by my side reminding me that life flows here. Quillan. I am here. Bright blue lampposts and a billboard showing me pictures of skiing and snow. What am I doing? I wanted sunshine, the billboards are lying, they are aged and faded to bluey whites by the sun. I smile. The mountains that looked impenetrable surround me now, like an evergreen hug. I have roamed and moved, lived, loved and lost. The man by my side is, has been and always was for life. We smile at each other knowing we are home.

That's how Quillan found me.

***

I am four or nearly five years old. The nuns are terrifying, apart from Sister Frances, she understands that I'm happy on the seesaw. But I don't stay long, my mother is too proud. Two little girls from a broken home have no place in a private Catholic convent.

Education did not cater for me. I gave it all I had but it had nothing for me. It did not matter because I could dance. I loved, I watched, I learned. I was loved and encouraged, you can be confident even if you can't spell it. When you are watched and feel the flow of movement of life you have achieved, by just knowing. At six I watched, I learned and I knew. My nan would say *She's a knowing child, not a know all.* The nans adored me, well two out of three and most children don't have that many nans! One nan and pa and both their mothers, two greats. The one great that was not such a fan was treated to a weekly recital of my not so good violin playing. She chose to stay in her room at the care home because she wasn't sitting with them all, waiting to die, so it was down to me; death by violin. My reward was a pre sucked toffee complete with fluff from the bottom of her handbag.

The other great nan would meet me and my sister in Margate and treat us to limeade and fish and chips too, if we were lucky. We would walk back together, she so sprightly in her late eighties.

I later learnt that she was a suffragette.There was a definite no nonsense attitude to complaining about lumps in the strawberry instant whip, and she would swear under her breath at the chiropodist. But I loved her stories of the dancehall days.

My nan, she is a book on her own. My biggest fan, with whom I shared a bond like no other. She was soft and cuddly, but strong as iron, with life advice that made it feel like you had thought of it for yourself. She looks over my shoulder as I write this, it is partly due to her that I am in Quillan. I am from a line of strong women, I wear their rings and keep a name of one of the great greats.

Tanned skin, tight burgundy curls, speed boats, water skiing, sailing, rugby, cycling, story teller, reliable, responsible; my grandpa. Stern, grumpy, funny, fit, supportive, musician, vulnerable. He died at seventy-five, just before my first child was born. Devastating.

My mum. Mums are always special, they gave us life. A special lady to be sure. If I were writing a book and not just a chapter I would tell you about her. I loved her and lost her but she got to be a nan to my three children. She was not treated fairly in life or love, but she held on to dignity and high heels.

You now know that I have three children: boy, boy, girl. *Have* may be the wrong word as I believe children and babies are only ever on loan. I am just a creator, designed to carry, give birth, nurture and provide the best support structure that I am able for another human to develop. I am twenty-three, living in Germany on a disused RAF base, with a husband who comes and goes. It's better when he's gone. Time for me to move on. I have moved house twenty-two times. I like moving and find myself rather good at it. It's like dancing, as long as you have planned well, know what you're dancing to and remembered your dancing shoes, what can go wrong? Nothing, because dance is all about being prepared, but most of all being prepared to improvise when the music changes and the dance goes on.

Quillan is move thirty-one. Nan's china has survived.

Our past shapes us but does not define us. I am and am not my past, but my past is part of me. I can liken mine to the contours on the walking map around Quillan: many many steep ups and not so gentle downs, and some foot paths that don't link up or just end.

Life can be a challenge, and challenged I have been. I walked too closely in my mother's shoes, until she was no more. This was when my dancing shoes went back on and I began to dance with life. Major chances were happening. I partnered my daughter, I knew my sons could dance alone, and would always be waiting in the wings.

I met and married, loved and lost again. I gained a large debt and a step son to nurture, although this dance was another one I needed to learn.

I knew my nan could not live for ever so the inevitable happened and there she was, gone at ninety-six, a good innings some may say, but she wanted her telegram from the queen. Now there is just me and my sister. I slowly realise that my nan has given me freedom. I've never had any money before. It's not a fortune but a comfortable cushion. Years before I had sold my jewellery to buy my daughter's school uniform. If I had told my nan she would have said *Needs must*, because even she was not aware of the comfortable cushion.

This inheritance is why I say my nan helped me to live in Quillan.

I still have some of my mother's high heels. I must have slipped them back on as I was to be directed to dance the hardest dance that nearly took my life. I didn't let it. I worked with every step and learnt that dance over and over. She wanted me to dance with her again, I had to say no I am not ready for my final curtain.

Quillan awaits me.

Susan's Story

I married very young. I was bullied at work. My best friend died. I found true love. I moved to France.

When I studied English at school I was taught that every story had a beginning, a middle and an end. It was also important to have some kind of structure to the story. I wasn't always very organised. I got carried away with my story with little thought about the ending. I remember one critique from an English teacher which went along the lines: *A very interesting story, with great characters, but the ending let you down.* I seem to remember it ended with: *And then they woke up and it was all a dream.* Not very original, I agree. Well, this story ends up like a dream, where I'm living in a beautiful little town in the South of France and I still can't quite believe it myself! So, how did it happen?

Getting out of your comfort zone can be quite uncomfortable, painful even. I'd worked in the same job for nineteen years, in the office of a Special School, starting part time and steadily increasing as my children got older. I was lucky enough to have had the luxury of being a full time mum from the time my eldest child was born until my youngest started school. For the most part, I loved my job. It was scary going back to work after a break of seven years. I had lost a lot of confidence in my abilities in the workplace. I shouldn't have worried as I was eased in gently, being interviewed (I say interviewed but it was more like a chat, a look around the school and a *When can you start?*) by the lovely, almost ready to retire, Headteacher.

What has any of this got to do with me deciding to get rid of most of my belongings, selling my house in Lancashire, leaving the country of my birth and moving to the South of France? It's hard to pinpoint when that decision was made, or even began as a seed in my mind. I've always found change difficult. I've realised that, through the years, I have taken a certain amount of comfort from knowing what the next day will bring. I've always loved holidays, days and nights out with friends and a certain amount of adventure, but I always felt more comfortable with the known rather than the unknown. I suppose that explains why I stayed for twenty-three years with a husband I married at twenty-one, even though for many years we lived as strangers in the same house. I remember that I was happy for the first part of the marriage and I loved being a mum and part of a family. However, I wasn't fully *me* at twenty-one and I grew into a person that didn't fit with my ex-husband. We grew in different directions and just didn't really like each other in the end. It turned out that we had completely different interests and a completely different sense of humour. Laughing is one of my favourite things, and we just didn't laugh about anything together. Luckily, for me, my children have inherited my unique sense of humour and we have always had a lot of fun together. I got used to my ex saying *You lot are weird*. For many years, I felt like a prisoner in my own home, walking on eggshells and worrying about what mood he would be in when he got home from work. He just didn't seem to like me at all, or at least the person I had become. But that was the real me and I felt guilty for changing. When my youngest child went through the usual teenage angst and stopped being his angelic princess he blamed me and told me, constantly, that it was my fault and that I was a bad mum. I started to believe it. I felt for many years that I was on my own, with no support and it was really hard. I was living in a house with a stranger who didn't like me. Like many people brought up as a Catholic, I thought that being married was for life and that there was no other option than to grin and bear it! And I was in my uncomfortable, comfort zone.

Back to work … as things got more difficult at home, I took comfort in work. I was good at it. It's hard for me to say that because I've never thought I was really good at anything. But I made some fantastic friends at work and they often told me how much I helped them, both at work and on a personal level. I've never thought I was great at giving advice, but people have always confided in me and trusted me. I felt like I had another family at work who really cared about me and when I'd had a terrible time at home, I could find respite in my work and my work friends.

Unfortunately, eventually, work life began to imitate home life. Looking back, it was me who changed and not work. I have always liked to be a people pleaser. I like to be liked. A combination of being good at my work, and trying to please people meant that when the new Headteacher took over a year or so after I started at the school, I was definitely in the good books. I think my new boss was impressed that I could read his appalling handwriting, guessed what he was trying to say when he was dictating and generally got things done without any fuss. When I was obviously upset about home life, he seemed so kind and understanding. I was surprised that many colleagues didn't share my views and, for the most part, had nothing very complimentary to say about him.

To cut a long story short, as soon as I disagreed with my boss, or refused, for example, to change the minutes of a meeting to suit him, he became a bully. Well, I'm certain he was always a bully, but now I was in the firing line. The change in his attitude towards me was immediate. I guess it took me a while to grow up and have my own voice. But I strongly believe in justice and I'd like to think I always stand up for the underdog, even at my own expense.

I always enjoyed working in an office, particularly in a school, where every day is different and being based in Reception, I enjoyed talking to visitors, staff and the children. I had no desire to become a Manager or to be involved in Finance. I knew that I could do it, as I had to frequently cover for the previous Office Manager when she was off on long term sickness, but I just didn't want to. So when the Office Manager eventually left (or was bullied out for daring to be sick), I didn't apply for the role and the Headteacher hired a new *confidante* who became my line manager and was paid very well to be a *yes man*. I was then basically bullied for many years. I carried on doing my job but bit by bit my confidence was crushed. I continued, for many years, to refuse to be a *yes man*, and to do my job to the best of my ability. It often made me physically and mentally sick, but still, it was my comfort zone.

I'm not sure what the final straw in my marriage was that broke the camel's back but I think I had subconsciously been waiting until my children had become adults before making a move to leave. I didn't have a very well paid job and had no idea how I would support two children on my own. When my youngest was eighteen I could no longer bear to live a half life, constantly anxious about how my other half was going to react to any given circumstance. Something seemingly insignificant could lead to a full blown argument. I couldn't stand the uncertainty and animosity any longer and suggested he let me have half the value of the house and in return I would leave, with just my favourite chair and a suitcase, along with my youngest child. My eldest, by this time, was living the majority of the time with a girlfriend.

Having left home to get married as a very young and innocent twenty-one year old, it was a huge change to own my own home. I had never had that kind of independence and although it was scary it was also incredibly liberating. No-one was telling me what to do and I didn't have to let anyone know where I was going or what time I would be home. For several years I really enjoyed being single. Life still had its ups and downs. There wasn't much money to spare and I was living with my daughter. She has turned out to be the most wonderful, beautiful, caring young woman. But I'm sure she would be the first to agree that she wasn't the easiest teenager to live with and we did have some very rocky times. I am, however, very blessed to have two incredible children who I am so proud of. If I've done something right in this life, then it is producing these two wonderful human beings!

I thought that I would never want to marry again or even have another relationship. That all changed six years after leaving my husband when I was invited to my beloved uncle's 80th birthday party. I was living in Lancashire and travelled to London to visit my folks, as I had done regularly since moving up north twenty years previously. On arriving at the party, I was immediately taken by a cousin, Liam, who I had briefly met on a few occasions growing up. We were, in fact, cousins in law. My dad's sister had married his dad's brother (my uncle, whose party it was!). We spent the whole evening playing like kids and making each other laugh. We even put on an impromptu show, leading to much eye rolling from both sides of the family. Eventually, just before he left to take his dad home, I said, in a slightly tipsy manner *You are gay, aren't you?* When he assured me that he was not I was slightly taken aback. That changed everything!

I thought the biggest move of my life was moving from London, where I was born, to Lancashire when I was twenty-five, pregnant and with a toddler in tow. I've always loved London, but when I was pregnant with my son I began to have panic attacks on the commute to work and regularly had to get off the tube during rush hour. My incredible bosses at the time, when I worked for Guinness in Central London, insisted that I come to work late and leave early during the latter part of my pregnancy. This, I think, was when I first thought about moving out of London. There were just too many people and I had a baby to think about now. My ex-husband was from Lancashire and we travelled *Up North* regularly to see his family. I loved the relaxed way of life and the countryside and the lack of crowds. So when I was pregnant with my second child, the idea of moving to Lancashire became even more appealing.

It was a much bigger shock than I had imagined. Firstly, while we were selling our flat in London, we decided to stay with my then mother-in-law. Fortunately we got on really well but it was a bit of a shock going from having my own car and access to regular tubes and buses to living in a village with no shops and a bus which went twice a day. The reality of being trapped with a toddler, whilst being pregnant was about to hit hard. In addition, I had left most of my family behind. I wasn't sure if I had actually made the right decision.

For many years I considered moving to Ireland, where I always felt so at home. We spent many summer and Christmas holidays at my Grandparents home in Northern Ireland and I always had a sense of coming home when I arrived on the island. I loved the smell of the burning turf and the sound of the river and the friendliness of the locals. As a teenager I found it strange and funny that no-one could walk past without saying something, whether it be *Hello*, or *How are you doing?* or even *It's wet!* (a slight understatement during a walk to the shop in torrential rain). Being brought up in London, this was a novelty, as it wasn't really the done thing to communicate with strangers. Once I'd had children though, it never really seemed to be the right time to consider moving. There was school and work to consider. I see a real similarity here in Quillan to the Ireland of my youth. People are really friendly and always say *Bonjour* or *Bonsoir* whenever you pass them in the street or enter a shop. (I haven't quite mastered the exact time that these salutations change from one to another!) There is also that sense of community where everyone seems to look out for each other. It's so refreshing after living in London where a lot of people (not all) try to avoid eye contact and even regard you with suspicion if you smile at them.

I'd been to France several times, firstly in my late teens, with colleagues from my first job, just on a day trip - mainly, I think, to get some cheap wine. My only real memory was going to the toilets and having to pass the men's urinals on the way. I'd never heard of communal toilets before. That was quite a shock. My ex-husband and I took the kids camping in the South of France when they were small, meeting up with some friends. What a terrible idea! Firstly I hated camping and secondly, we travelled for several hours, passing some really beautiful villages on the way, just to arrive at a dry, uninspiring campsite, in August. What was I thinking? It was so hot that we spent most of the day in the air conditioned Hypermarket, only daring to go to the beach in the early evening so that myself and my two ginger children didn't burn to death. We were also attacked every evening by some very large flying insects that we had to bat away with our badminton rackets. Not a great holiday.

We did the usual trip to Disneyland Paris when the kids were a bit older and, of course, the kids wanted McDonalds. I was always in the bottom set at school for French, but I managed to remember *sans fromage* whilst ordering my burger! Imagine moving to France and not liking cheese? Another memory was forcing my kids to walk up several hundred steps to see the *Sacre Coeur* in Montmartre. They were disgusted that after all that walking up hundreds of steps there was only a church at the top and they refused to go in. My sister and I celebrated my 40th birthday in Paris which was a lot of fun, but, as my birthday is at the end of July, we were surprised that many bars and restaurants were closing for the summer. We found out that this is the norm. Still, we had fun for the next few days trying different cocktails and eating burgers at the Hard Rock Cafe (which remained open during our visit). So I didn't exactly have the most amazing experiences in France and moving there was never at the top of my list of things to do - not even on the list!

My uncle's birthday party was a pivotal moment in my life I now realise. After hitting it off so well with Liam, we stayed in touch with increasingly long phone calls, him living in London and me in Lancashire. Whenever I visited London to see my folks, we would get together and we soon became *an item*. Long distance relationships are difficult but neither of us were in a position to move.

One day, about two years into our relationship, I rang him on my lunch break, which was a daily occurrence. I've never been a big fan of talking on the phone but with Liam it was different. We never ran out of anything to say and we laughed a lot. We still do thankfully. It was a seemingly ordinary day, in that, my boss was up to his usual tricks of trying to upset me for no apparent reason. School had just started back in September and the first thing he did was to send my Line Manager in to remind me and my colleague to be *respectful* and *professional* at all times. This would have been funny, coming from him at any other time, but on that day I had just had enough. I had always been respectful and professional to everyone who visited the school, unlike him, so I was understandably furious that he had sent this *message* instead of coming into the office himself or even the fact that he felt it was necessary to say it at all.

I mentioned this to Liam on our daily lunch time chat, and I guess he had just heard too many similar stories from me over the last few years. He told me to hand my notice in and leave. Of course, I couldn't do that, I'd been in the job for nineteen years, and for the most part, loved it, and what would I do instead, where would I go? I had put up with much more in the past from this bully. I had only intended to sound off. But no, Liam, uncharacteristically, insisted, saying that he'd had enough of my boss' bullying and I wasn't to stand for it anymore. I should leave my job and come and live with him in London. He was adamant!

I got back to work after lunch and the idea kept going around in my head. I was so sick of being treated badly by my boss. He seemed to deliberately try and upset me on a daily basis. I could go into detail about all the ways he tried to upset and undermine me but, to be honest, that would give him far more airtime than he deserves. Suffice to say, after some deliberation, I decided to hand my notice in there and then, much to his surprise. He had tried for years to make work so unbearable for me that I would leave and here I was handing it to him on a plate. I told him I no longer wanted to be treated so badly and that I didn't deserve it. Of course, he didn't want to take the blame and so informed the rest of the staff in the afternoon staff briefing that I was leaving to move to London, an assumption he had made as he knew that I had family, and now a boyfriend in London. There was no way that he was going to give the real reason. I'm fairly sure that whilst making this false statement he pulled at the skin on his turkey neck, something he did whenever he was caught out or was lying - so pretty much all of the time.

A few months after I had left and moved to London to live with Liam and his father, I returned to Lancashire to see my kids and some friends. I was invited to a colleagues' retirement party and I was delighted to attend. I'd had a few drinks (I have to admit) and this may have given me a little Dutch courage, so I decided to walk up to my ex-boss (who was propping up the bar as usual as if he owned the place). He looked a little surprised to see me. *I just wanted to thank you for being such a bully,* I said. This didn't please him at all and he started to stutter and pull at his turkey neck, saying *You can't say that!* But I could say whatever I wanted and I continued to thank him for continuously being a bully because if he hadn't I wouldn't have had the courage to leave my job and my home. I was now blissfully happy with my boyfriend and had a job in a school where the Headteacher and all the staff appreciated me. It was the best thing that could have happened. It was true. And he was furious and I must say that pleased me immensely. I did regret having this conversation at the party as it was not the most appropriate setting but I couldn't pass up the opportunity as I knew I would hopefully never have to see him again.

Life wasn't immediately great once I'd handed my notice in. Reality hit me and I realised that I had given up a steady job, with a good pension and I really had no idea what was going to happen next. Liam was absolutely brilliant, as were my family. I had a very stressful few months where I lost all my confidence. I couldn't imagine starting a new job and I was really scared. My daughter had already been living with me at my house in Lancashire and my son decided to move in too when I moved out. This wasn't ideal, as, although my kids adore each other, they didn't find it particularly easy living together without me being a referee. But it paid the mortgage and that was one thing less to worry about.

I had a few very difficult weeks in London and suffered quite badly with my mental health. Even though I was living with Liam (who was absolutely amazing and reassured me daily) and I was close to my parents, I just couldn't seem to cope with life. I was scared of everything. I couldn't imagine ever working again and my confidence was at an all time low. Everyone was telling me how brave I was and how exciting my life was going to be but I found it hard to even get up in the morning. Amazingly, about a month later I found the courage to contact an agency and within a week I was working at a school near to my parents' house in London. I was supposed to be filling in while they looked for a new administrator, but on the day of the interviews, after asking my views on all the candidates, they told me they liked me the best and without having to have an interview they offered me the job. I was just delighted as I had already made some lovely new friends at the school and it meant I didn't have to start all over again at another temping role.

I spent two fantastic years living with Liam and his dad. Liam was his full time carer. I was also near to my parents and my sister who I could now see regularly. I am so lucky that I have a fantastic relationship with my sister. We are such good friends and she is one of the funniest and kindest people I know. She couldn't wait to come out to visit us in Quillan and she instantly fell in love with our home. She has already planned her third visit and I can't wait. She has a very stressful job and a busy life, especially now she has three grandchildren who she adores (and vice versa) so when she comes here she can just relax and enjoy the beautiful countryside and the slower pace of life. I'm still hoping that when she retires she'll buy the house next door.

When circumstances changed and Liam's dad had to go into a home we had to leave the house in London and the only reasonable thing to do was move back to Lancashire. This was a mixed blessing. It was wonderful to be near my kids again and I got to see my old friends. However I was restless. This seemed like a backward move. Liam and I had already discussed selling the house and moving somewhere else - a home that would be ours. We talked long and hard about the possibility of moving to Ireland but prices had risen so much and the weather was no better than England and I suffer from Seasonal Affective Disorder. We toyed with the idea of moving to different parts of the UK, including Bristol as it seemed very arty and interesting. We both secured temping roles back in Lancashire and decided to decorate the house in preparation for selling. We were getting more and more disillusioned with Britain and its politics. And then Brexit happened. This was a disaster and we both decided we had to get out.

Having ruled out Ireland, we began to look further afield. Liam's brother had moved to France a few years previously and he and his wife absolutely loved it. In one of our telephone conversations with them, after a few glasses of wine, we started wondering if we too could make the move. It all seemed very *pie in the sky* to start with but the more we talked about it, the more excited we got. Could we really do it? One day it would seem the ideal solution, and the next I was filled with angst and a long list of reasons why it couldn't work. I was terrible at French, I wondered how we would survive and what work we would be able to do without knowing the language? But the more we spoke about it, and the more research we did, it became more of a possibility. Everyone we spoke to about it was full of encouragement and envy, often saying it was something they always dreamed of. We were both working in temporary jobs so I think that made the decision a little easier and both my kids had left home at this stage. Many people asked how we were going to manage to make the move after Brexit. This is where I became a little smug and said that the first thing I did after it was announced was to apply for my Irish passport - thank you Mum and Dad. Liam's parents were also Irish and he had held his Irish passport for many years.

So we started looking at properties in Quillan and the surrounding area, before we had even been there on holiday. We loved everything we saw, heard and read about the area. We came to stay with Liam's brother and sister-in-law for a holiday and instantly fell in love with Quillan. It was so beautiful, surrounded by mountains and with a multitude of wildlife. Liam is a keen bird watcher and just couldn't believe what an amazing place it was for wildlife. We could both immediately imagine ourselves living here. So, we looked at several houses during that holiday but, although there were some within our price range, nothing really caught our eye. We were told that outdoor space was essential if you were going to be living here all year round.

When we returned to England we carried on our search, daily scouring every property site we could. We liked the look of one house that was beautifully decorated, in a great position in town but with only a balcony and no other outdoor space. We convinced ourselves that that would be enough for us as we would only be a minute's walk from the river. We arranged to come back to Quillan to view the property, fell in love with it immediately and put in an offer. We put our house up for sale and started selling everything. We had no intention of bringing anything with us. It was a brand new start. After a few weeks back and forth with the agent, we were informed that a cash buyer had come along and made an offer on our dream house and they had accepted. I was so upset and felt that we'd never find anything as good.

Liam didn't give up hope and kept searching every day and sending me photos and descriptions whilst on his break at work. I discarded everything until one day he sent me some photos and I immediately perked up. This looked interesting. We asked for more details and photos and found out that the location was perfect and it had a terrace and a yard. We were sold. Not wanting to risk losing another house, we asked Liam's brother, sister-in-law and a friend to go and look at it for us. When they all loved it we put an offer in straight away - without actually seeing it. Luckily when we did come to see it a few weeks later we instantly fell in love with it. We feel so blessed that the first house fell through. We want this to be our forever home and will do whatever we can to make that happen. I feel that this is where we are meant to be. Almost a year later, we both wake up every day and want to pinch ourselves to see if this is in fact real.

Live every day as if it is your last. This was very much the attitude of my very close friend Alison. We worked together for ten years, me in the school office and her as a Teaching Assistant. We had the same, silly sense of humour and spent many weekends away together. Sometimes we would just go out for the day and would end up deciding to stay the night, grabbing a toothbrush from the local shop. If Alison decided to do something, she would just make it happen. We'd be chatting over a glass of wine, or three, in the local pub and she'd suddenly say something like *Let's go to Amsterdam!* Then the laptop would come out and she'd be booking it. She was so organised and loved to plan everything down to the last detail, which I loved because it saved me doing it.

When everything around me was going wrong, including my marriage and being bullied at work, Ali was my saviour. We had the best times together. She always said *Let's have something to look forward to* and, true to her word, we always planned a holiday, a weekend away or even a night out. She was an absolute joy. I've always hated shopping but she loved it and would persuade me to come shopping with her by promising to take me to the wine bar with twinkly lights in Preston, or *Prestonia* as she liked to call it, to make it sound more exotic. It wasn't!

Ali and I had several holidays together. Apart from weekends away in the UK; Shrewsbury was a favourite, we travelled together to Italy, Amsterdam and New York. We had plans to go back to Italy, to Bergamo, which we both absolutely loved and also to go to Austria, a country I have never been to.

A few weeks before our planned holiday to Bergamo, Ali was on a mountain climbing holiday with her husband. One sunny afternoon, during the long summer holidays (one of the perks of working in a school) I got a call which would have a huge impact on my life. I'd been drinking cocktails in a friend's garden when I got a phone call to tell me Ali had fallen off a mountain and died. Now, this information just didn't sink in. How could this be true? My beautiful, vibrant friend, always so full of life. It just wasn't possible.

Life after that was pretty much a blur for quite a long time. I went into meltdown. I was on the verge of leaving my husband, having made the huge decision to leave, which, although I knew was the only thing I could do, was incredibly scary. A few days after hearing that my best friend had tragically died, the house I was buying fell through so I was forced to remain living with my ex- husband. You can only imagine how uncomfortable that was and I was also unable to eat, sleep or function in any way. Such a dark, dark time. I missed her so much and was so incredibly sad. I must have listened to her last answerphone message that she'd left me a hundred times. She was so good at leaving really long messages. I would dial up and pretend she was talking to me. She told me how much she was looking forward to our holiday in Italy and talked about going to Wales and to Austria. One day, several weeks later, I rang my answerphone message service and the message had disappeared and it felt like losing her all over again.

As I mentioned Ali was very organised, and always lived life to the full. One thing I'm grateful for was that she always set out to do as much as she could. If she wanted to go somewhere she would make it happen. When you lose someone so close it really does make you re-evaluate life. Sometimes you just have to get on and do it. I've always been very good at deliberating and putting things off. I think Ali would be so proud of me making the decision to live out my dream, get out of my comfort zone and move to somewhere so beautiful. I think she would also have been a bit annoyed that it didn't happen in her lifetime. She would have loved it here. But I'm reminded of her daily. Every time I see a beautiful butterfly (and there are many here in Quillan) I nod to the sky, smile and say *Cheers Ali.*

A couple of years after Alison died, and not long after I had started seeing Liam, we planned a holiday together in the Lake District. We had booked into a lovely country pub that did bed and breakfast. It looked idyllic and was in a beautiful spot in the Lakes called Eskdale. We were looking forward to long walks in the countryside. We planned out a route and I was driving in my beloved VW Beetle. Unlike Alison, I don't always plan ahead, so it hadn't occurred to me that we would be up in the mountains and my SatNav may not work. Of course I had no map. I've never been able to read one and always relied on the SatNav on my phone. Liam had travelled up North to meet me after work so it was beginning to get dark en route. All was going swimmingly and we were so excited to have a rare weekend away together. Then the SatNav stopped working. I wasn't too concerned at first as I thought I could just follow signs to Eskdale. However, it turns out that there are two very different ways to get there. And of course I had chosen the wrong one. We managed to find a petrol station and bought a map. We were already in the Lake District by now so we asked the guy behind the counter if he could recommend a route for us. He looked a bit sheepish and told us there were two ways to get there but we'd have to turn back on ourselves to get there on the easier route. The quickest way would be to go through Hardknott Pass and he indicated it on the map. Liam is good at reading maps so I was a little concerned but not overly. We had a map to follow now. What could go wrong? Welcome to the steepest road in England! Oh dear God. I have never been so frightened in my entire life (and I had survived teenagers). It was now pitch black and we found ourselves driving up the steepest, windiest, single tracked, scariest road I could ever imagine. All I could think of were the last words to my daughter where I promised that I wouldn't fall off a mountain on the holiday. (Alison's death had a big effect on her too). My headlights were just shining up into the sky and I had no clue what the road ahead looked like. All I could see was a sheer drop to the side of the road. There would have been no chance of passing if a car had been coming in the opposite direction. And sure, who would be mad enough to be driving over Hardknott Pass in the dark? Liam was the most wonderful co-driver and guide and he spoke to me and reassured me in the calmest manner, although I'm sure it did cross his mind that I was going to kill us both. Liam has always been a keen cyclist and doesn't drive. I cannot explain how terrified I was and my knuckles were white from grasping the steering wheel. When a sheep stepped in front of me I just froze and couldn't even find the horn to make him move. When he eventually sauntered off I had to do the best hill start of my life. After what felt like days, we eventually got over the mountain, going at a top speed of about two miles per hour. According to Liam and his map, the destination was only a few minutes away. We saw the lights ahead, after the now pitch black night around us and I indicated right into the Car Park. I stopped the car and Liam had to peel my fingers off the wheel. After telling me how amazing I was to get us there safely, Liam asked *Aren't you going to park the car properly? No I'm never getting back in it again*, was my response as I abandoned my beloved Betty (my Beetle) in the middle of the Car Park. I entered the Pub, and headed for Reception like a Zombie. The Receptionist took one look at me and asked *Did you come over Hardknott Pass?* I nodded. *In the dark?* I nodded again. *The bar is that way*, she said, sympathetically.

We never went abroad for our holidays when I was a child. But we had the best holidays ever. We went to Devon, Cornwall, Dorset and Ireland - funny that I don't class Ireland as abroad - it was just where the family were from. One of my favourite destinations was Westward Ho! Looking back there wasn't a huge amount to do. Of course we went to the beach, got sunburnt, put on calamine lotion, the usual. We thought it was a great treat to go to the Wimpy, especially if we had a milkshake or a banana split. The evening's entertainment was usually sitting in the local pub with a bottle of coke and a bag of crisps and putting a few coins in the jukebox. As time went on, things got really exciting with the introduction of night time entertainment, a highlight being Leslie on the organ. I remember going to Devon the year that the *Wurzles* had a hit with *I am a Cider Drinker* and my Dad thought it was hilarious to embarrass my sister and I by putting on a Cornish accent and ordering a pint of cider. I remember that he tried to embarrass us a lot but he was incredibly funny and I appreciated his sense of humour more and more as I got older. I like to think I got my sense of humour from my Dad. I had a wonderful childhood and cherished our holidays together as a family. The sun always seemed to shine.

Although we didn't venture far from home as children, we still experienced the wider world through our many lodgers. When I was born we lived on one floor of a large Victorian house, sharing one bedroom with my parents and my sister. When I was a teenager, my parents managed to buy the house, with a sitting tenant on the top floor. A few years later, we had the whole house, and to help pay the bills we took in lodgers on the top floor. These were mainly Australians, who seemed to love Shepherds Bush. I absolutely loved having lodgers. They always seemed so exotic. We made friends with them and they would often become part of the family, even babysitting for us sometimes. And there were a lot of parties. There was always a welcome for everyone in my family home growing up. My Mum and Dad were so generous and such great hosts. Everyone wanted to come to the house and everyone was fed well. All our friends wanted to be honorary children as our parents were so cool. When the lodgers went on their numerous trips around Europe they would always bring back goodies. I especially liked all the unusual sweets from different countries. I always loved the idea of being able to travel when I was older.

My Uncle worked for Dupont and when I was in my late teens he was transferred to America for a few years with his family. I desperately wanted to go and visit and started looking into working over there as an *Au pair*. The idea of living abroad, but with family nearby, terrified but excited me. I then met my future husband and all thoughts of leaving the UK were abandoned. I was relieved to be honest.

When I met Liam I discovered a new love for travel. He had travelled extensively since he was a teenager and has lived in several different countries. We would regularly discuss places we had both been and places we would love to go to. We discovered that we had always both wanted to go to Iceland. Neither of us had much money and we both had family and work commitments but we did some research and managed to get a last minute holiday, very cheap, staying in a Youth Hostel. It was one of the best holidays I have ever had and my thirst for travel was reignited. Another country that we had always wanted to go to was Morocco. We bought travel books and had great fun planning what we'd do if we ever managed to go. An incredibly cheap offer popped up on my daily search for an all inclusive holiday in Marrakesh a week before Christmas one year. We were just about to move back to Lancashire, had no jobs but decided to go anyway. We might never get the chance again. It was very different to our holiday in Iceland. This was luxury for us and I'm not sure I'd ever do it again but what a great experience. It was like a high class Butlins. We threw ourselves into all the entertainment, being thrilled at winning a certificate for *Boules* and Liam was a hit at the Karaoke. A day in the Atlas mountains made the whole trip worthwhile. It was breathtaking. A truly amazing experience.

The Souk that I had been so looking forward to was a bit of a nightmare. There were so many people and everyone wanted to grab hold of you and entice you to eat or have a snake wrapped around your neck or a henna tattoo. It was all a bit too much for me! But I had the travel bug and we managed to get cheap last minute holidays to Greece, where Liam taught me how to swim underwater and a whole new world opened up for me when I went snorkelling in the warm sea for the first time ever (in my 50s). It was truly incredible. I realised there was a whole world out there waiting to be discovered.

Moving to Quillan has been the bravest thing I have ever done. People kept saying that to me and I think it's true. It was a brave move. I sold practically everything I owned before moving here. It was very hard. I spent hours, days, months sifting through paperwork, photographs and my children's memorabilia. That was tough. Selling and donating furniture etc was hard work but not as emotionally draining. When I arrived in Quillan to spend the first night in our new home it was very cold and we couldn't turn on the gas. I did wonder what on earth I had done. But the next day, even though it was still cold, the sun was shining on a new day and we got the heating to work. It's not been plain sailing since then. There was a lot to sort out. As anyone who knows anything about France is well aware, there is a lot of paperwork. It's difficult enough moving home and setting up bills etc when it's in your own language, but it's very tough when you have very little knowledge of French (even after two years of daily Duolingo practice). I've had a few wobbles, wondering if we can make it work, make enough money to survive and avoid paying any fines for unpaid taxes, but I know we absolutely made the right decision. And after nearly a year in our new home, I can honestly say it really is a dream come true. I hope this will be my forever home. I'm surrounded by the beauty of nature, living right next to the river and my mental health has improved dramatically. The local people have been an absolute joy and we have made so many friends already. Everyone wants the best for you and are so willing to help and advise. I honestly feel blessed that my story, so far, has ended in Quillan. I took you on a bit of a roundabout journey, but we got there in the end. Not sure my English Teachers would have been impressed with the unstructured story, but hopefully I'd get points for effort.

Christine's Story

More Than Just A Song

July 2023

The sun has caught me right away. Finally, it's here. Even though in about half an hour, I'll have to put up the sunshade again because it relentlessly shines directly onto the terrace, I'm relishing these first rays. I've been sitting here for a while, like every morning. Early, when the sun rises behind us, I'm fascinated by its play of light with the mountains opposite, and when I spot a vulture circling, everything in this world feels right.

Every day is different but always overwhelming.

Like every morning, the coffee I drink on this terrace viewing this panorama tastes incomparable. And like every morning and every day, the sound of the River Aude fills me with joy and emotions that only nature can ignite within me. If I were musically inclined, its song would be my own symphony. The tranquility behind the rush. Being with myself and within myself. The best place in the world to find peace within yourself.

The closest thing to crazy.

And the best place in the world to figure out: What do I really want. Now, for the last big chapter of my life? Germany and Berlin with all its doubters, complainers, its hustle while simultaneously at a standstill (a dubious achievement) – so far away, cut off. But how to deal with the feelings of missing the children, family, friends. Good food, culture, abundance, endless opportunities.

September 2021

Our camper, *Huddel* purrs! Finally, we're on the road again, traveling through France. For two years, we've been planning this, always something was getting in the way. Bad weather, diverting us to Italy. Covid, limiting us to the German North Sea.

The dream of a house in the South, a life in warmth and light, has been within me for ages. Tassilo has known my thoughts from the beginning, and if he hadn't been so open and flexible in the nineteen years we've known each other, who knows if we would have made it this far together.

For weeks before the trip, I was doing my favourite hobby: checking real estate listings. Just like that. For fun. Just taking a look. Getting information. Which region is *nice*, which one is underrated. Where can one afford something at all? What are the living costs in France, what are the additional costs? What's the tax situation?

The Loire, too far from the sea. Normandy, Brittany, too cold and wet. The Atlantic coast, too expensive. Alsace has many beautiful, affordable offers. But I don't want Alsace, too close to Germany. Cote d'Azur, too posh (and too expensive), Provence… my dream. But unaffordable for us. Then I discovered this one blog which was listing the Aude area as a hidden gem. I delved deeper into this recommendation, studied property offers, and thought for the first time: *hey, this is interesting. This area suits us.*

Now I have a small list of properties, three or four viewing appointments with agents. As we travel through France, we'll look at houses in the countryside, with gardens, to refurbish and renovate. A new project will come at some point; this is an initial exploration. Who knows if and when it will become real, but it's just fun to dabble in half-real dreams!

We plan our camper trip around this activity. We'll pause in Paris, cycle through the city, admire the wrapped L'Arc de Triomphe (a bird dropping compared to our Wrapped Reichstag), travel down the Atlantic coast. The Aude department, as I researched beforehand, is a hidden gem. An underrated area, lots of potential, the new Provence. For people willing to take a chance, who know how to live but don't have millions to spare. Who can wait and watch how things evolve. Just right for us. So, after visiting the Atlantic coast, our journey will continue through this department to the Mediterranean.

Capbreton, Plage des Oceanides. How cool, we get a coveted spot right by the dunes. Good thing we arrived early. It's getting really crowded now. Young people, surfers, young families. A great, free parking lot, right by the beautiful beach, where campers are allowed to stay overnight. Exactly the atmosphere I love. For a short time, you can imagine yourself being completely free and unattached, no everyday constraints, just wind, sand, waves, blue sky.

We spend ages at the local bar *Soweto* and watch the spectacular sunset. It becomes a get-together, a shared moment of amazement, pausing together. Many people in a peaceful mood.

The night is less pleasant for us. Tassilo seems to have caught a virus and spends more time on the toilet than in bed. We decide not to travel to Aude as planned but to get medication and stay another day at this parking lot. He needs rest.

The route for the next day is set. We'll make a detour to the town of Espelette to buy *Piment d'Espelette*, where it's produced. Then, we'll head straight to the Aude valley, where at lunchtime we've arranged our first viewing appointment in a place called Quillan. Quillan's campsite has good Google reviews, and the town has good infrastructure, so we'll use it as a base for our excursions to agent offers in small surrounding villages.

Tassilo sleeps, I google for more properties again and suddenly see a new listing from an agent I hadn't discovered before. Well, not what I wanted: no garden, not for renovation. But very chic. A small townhouse in great condition. The highlight is a terrace overlooking the Aude River. Unfortunately, it's priced above budget. But for some reason, I'm intrigued. Tassilo wakes up: *Look honey, I found something else in the town of Quillan where we're staying tomorrow. A townhouse with a terrace. Take a look, it's a bit overpriced, but interesting. We could check it out. What do you think?* Tassilo: *Looks great, set up an appointment with the real estate agent.* I message the agent and ask for a callback.

The second night in Capbreton is also restless. Tassilo still isn't feeling quite well. When he finally settles down to sleep - it's half past one in the morning - I'm still awake, unable to sleep. I spontaneously decide not to go to the chosen campsite in Quillan the next day. We need some comfort. A bathroom, decent toilets, a bedroom instead of a bunk bed in the camper. During the night, I find a lovely room in a private accommodation hosted by Jo and Matthew on Airbnb and send an inquiry. A good decision. In the morning, the confirmation comes through, and we set off.

During the drive - Tassilo is finally feeling better - I delve deeper into this area. I read aloud interesting facts about Quillan, the highlights of the region, and descriptions of the local nature. We're filled with anticipation. Inexplicable, actually. At 3:00 pm, we have the first appointment with the agent, the only one that day. We plan to check in at the Airbnb around noon, rest a bit, and then walk to the agent's office. Small town. Everything within walking distance, as the map shows.

On the way, we pass through Nébias, a village where we're supposed to have another viewing the next day. We briefly stop and explore the two or three streets. No café/bar, zero infrastructure, not even a tiny grocery store... My husband is horrified. *Well, I wouldn't want to live here. It's completely isolated, what would one do here all day?*

Well, we're quite different, he and I. I love peace, seclusion, and solitude. But, and this valid question I have to honestly ask myself: *Do I always love it? Me, a born Berliner, could I actually live in permanent seclusion?* I'm disillusioned and uncertain about what I really want and can "endure." I notice that all the scheduled appointments for properties are similar to that one of Nébias. And the real estate agent I asked to call back regarding the townhouse in Quillan hasn't contacted me. Tassilo calls her again on his mobile, requesting a callback. Well, otherwise, these viewings will just remain a nice travel activity, nothing more.

The road from Nébias to Quillan - what an experience! Such impressive switchbacks amid the characteristic Pyrenean vegetation that suddenly and unexpectedly reveals the vast, spectacular view of the small town. Breathtaking! We park at both stopping points. We stand there, look at each other, both speechless and amazed. At that moment, our love for this place begins to grow. We're full of anticipation for the next three days we've planned.

Huddel squeezes through Quillan's narrow streets. I'm anxious, worried about our camper. My husband always takes the smallest streets, no matter how big the car is. A parking spot is always sought right in front of the house, even as the one-way streets get more and more narrow. Puh…Exciting. Finally, we arrive at a lovely spot, park, and walk to our accommodation. It's supposed to be right by the Aude River, as the photos suggested. However, the entrance is on the street side, and after a brief search, we stand in front of the house and ring the bell.

Hostess Jo opens the door, and I immediately think: how nice, how warm. How good it is that we didn't go to the campsite. We settle into our room, chat downstairs in the kitchen with her, and briefly enjoy the terrace by the river. An engaging conversation starts right away. What a likeable woman - but we have to cut it short due to the upcoming appointment with the agent, as we inform her. *Ah, you're looking for a house here? I know of a really beautiful house that's for sale. Right across the river, on the other side. I know the sellers. If you'd like, I can make the connection, and I'm sure you can visit it, it is that one over there.* She points across the river... to a small, tiny, orange townhouse with a small terrace on the top floor. I'm electrified: *Tassilo, this is the property from the agent who hasn't called us back! What a coincidence!* Coincidence or sign? We ask Jo to establish contact with the sellers.

Now we head to our first appointment with the real estate agent. The viewing turns out to be a big disappointment. Poor condition, busy location. Lots of work, uncertain right of way. Absolutely unacceptable.

Back at our accommodation, our hostess has actually arranged a viewing of the townhouse for us in the afternoon. The real estate agent hasn't got in touch so far. And never will.

We walk across Place de la République, cross the old bridge for the first time, enjoying the views on both sides. The Aude, this river that gives the department its name, fascinates us. So powerful yet elegantly flowing past the old town.

The house we're viewing is small. Very small. Tiny. We ring the bell, and the owners, Jane and Simon, open the door. The house is so small that the two of them have to move into the bedroom to let us in. I seem obviously surprised because the seller jokingly remarks: *It gets wider as you go up.* The house is small but delightful and in a fantastic, newly renovated condition. The bedroom with an ensuite bathroom, something I've always wanted. On the middle floor, the living room — a fireplace — something I've always wanted. The highlight on the top floor is the terrace, connected to the open kitchen with bi-fold doors that span the entire length of the room. The terrace thus becomes an extension of the kitchen-dining area. A dream. And then the view from the terrace of the river and the opposite mountains, where the vultures have their home, where the morning light catches the cliffs and the sun sets in the evenings. Impressive.

We are both overwhelmed and independently feel: This could be it. The feeling is right. If anything, this is it. We don't need to look any further.

During dinner at *La Galerie*, we both hardly realise what we're eating. It's unimportant. We talk about nothing other than this house and this little town Quillan. It's not what I wanted. I wanted a house with a garden. A detached house, somewhere remote... but this house has struck a chord within me, and my intuition tells me not to search further. Tassilo feels the same, and whatever comes of this interest, whether we can actually afford the house and really move in the end, we won't look at any other properties. I cancel the remaining appointments.

It's not on our agenda, at this time, to buy a house so quickly, to change our place of residence. How would we even finance it, what are the loan options, the work situation? I call my bank, request a callback. We agreed with the sellers to sleep on it for a night, to come back the next day to address further questions. They are very nice, and we have a good feeling. We decide to extend our stay in Quillan to get a better sense of the place.

Before we return to our accommodation, we explore a few more streets in the town. The church, illuminated in warm light, the Place de la République as well, and some people sitting outside, the plane trees, and the water feature — we are enchanted. Briefly passing *our* house once more in the dark... We cross the Pont Suzanne — my sister's name is Susanne — and see that as another sign. If you want to see signs, you'll see them.

The night is restless, sleeping almost impossible. I'm full of adrenaline, excitement, afraid of my own boldness. What an enormous, life-altering step this could be! I feel sick from the rush of emotions, battling, spreading within me. I keep getting up, leaving the bedroom, and going to the window in the living room that overlooks the house. Directly across. Only the Aude River between us. The Aude, now dark and loud. The rush of water cascading along the rocks seems immense, deep, threatening tonight? And loud, incredibly loud. The windows are shut, yet this underlying hum is ever-present. You can't escape it. That gives me pause, it makes me doubt if that house across the way is truly the right choice. What if I can't bear the noise in the long run, if I'm always and constantly exposed to it? In Berlin, I have to cope with the highway behind the house — do I really want to exchange that for a different but ultimately similar sound? Will I get used to it? Could I possibly reach a point where I can't live without this noise?

I pace through the living room, sit for a while in the cozy armchairs. Make myself a nighttime tea to calm down. Then, with the tea in hand, I approach the piano sitting in the huge room, possibly inviting someone to play. Not at night, and I'm not the right person for playing, but it looks inviting. A beautiful picture. I sit on the stool in front of it, observing the open sheet music placed on the stand:

Closest Thing to Crazy (Katie Melua)

A twist of fate? A sign. Definitely an incredible coincidence. There are millions of songs that could be open here. I stare at the notes and simply can't believe it is THIS song. Finally, I go to bed, and finally, I can sleep.

26th August 2006

My sister takes the microphone and addresses us and our guests. The official part of our wedding is over, all speeches have been given, the food was — as we were told — delicious. (Which couple can actually remember the food and drinks years later?) *Dear Tini, dear Tassilo. We've prepared something for you and hope you'll like it. Lights out, film on.*

Pictures and old Super8 film sequences of us as babies, toddlers, adults. Individually, with parents, sister, as a loving couple, looking cool with sunglasses, always looking good (she chose the right pictures), as a family with our two adorable children. The perfect patchwork family. Then, interviews on the street with passersby, how they individually assess us, how they think our marriage will go, whether we'll have more children. My sister and her partner, both professional filmmakers, have made a touching, humorous, simply fantastic film about us.

And throughout this film, Katie's song *Closest Thing to Crazy* underscores our story, our love. How did my sister know that this is our song, that we've listened to it loudly, repeatedly at home, feeling so connected? We're speechless, touched, and incredibly happy.

September 2021

Alcohol isn't the reason I feel utterly terrible. It feels like a truck ran over me, I have headaches from thinking, I'm totally exhausted, barely capable of having a morning conversation with Matthew. I can't enjoy his delicious breakfast, I can't eat anything. There's a whirlwind in my stomach, I feel sick. It's like butterflies in the stomach. That brief moment before realising you've fallen in love, that's how it feels.

We spend the day in town, exploring the infrastructure, discovering the area. It's very quiet, very little going on. Covid seems to have had a significant impact here. Many shops had to close; the high season with many activities and festivals is from June/July to mid-September, as we're repeatedly told. We're too late for everything and experience Quillan as drowsy, with possibly a lot of potential but currently with a slightly morbid charm. Tassilo actually needs life, action, variety. A different restaurant every day. Art, culture, pubs, bars. I'm unsure if this is really right for him, if he can endure it here for long.

Back at the Airbnb, Jo welcomes us so warmly that it feels like we've been here forever, like we've known each other forever. For the evening, she invites us to an informal gathering on the terrace with some friends, all expats from different parts of the world. She tells us how they came to Quillan, what life is like here, why they live here. I ask her for her honest assessment of the house and the situation in the area, posing many practical questions. The conversation with her does us a world of good, and when we head over to our second meeting with Jane and Simon at the Pouzadou house, we have a small list of important points we still want to clarify.

The second encounter with Jane and Simon and *our* house is clarifying, and we're happy that the first impression, the initial feeling, has been confirmed. All points can be constructively discussed; all information is readily provided. The two, it seems to us, are uncomplicated, trustworthy, open, and honest. The little house is simply a dream; we like it even better the second time. The quality of its renovation is exceptional. You can move in immediately; there's nothing to do. Some furniture will be left; a sofa bed, terrace furniture, and some chandeliers - they belong here, surprisingly, they suit this environment and will remain. Eventually, all questions are asked, everything important is said, and we have to leave. Even though we'll submit the written letter of intent the very next day, it will still take several months before we can take over the house.

The Aude rushes and boils, but it's quieter here than on the opposite side. It's a pleasant background murmur, and I already find it relaxing. I'm relieved. We say goodbye to Jane and Simon and feel like they consider us worthy buyers, and the four of us could become more than just seller-buyer. It's a small, moving farewell when we leave, telling them: *We're sure, this is it. We feel so comfortable in the house, and we've also fallen in love with the place, even though there isn't much happening.*

We head to dine at the *Platane*. Okay, gastronomically, the place has potential for improvement. Coming from Berlin, the expectations one has of a restaurant are probably too high. We need to learn to live and dine in a small town.

The evening on Jo and Matthew's terrace becomes a final highlight. Among the expatriates living in Quillan — Americans, a Spaniard, a Frenchman, Englishmen, and us two Germans in between — it's such a fun, carefree evening that once again opens our hearts to the place. We've arrived. We're welcomed. We're grounded. Sometimes you meet people to whom you feel immediately drawn, connected. As if something is vibrating in the air, an affinity that creates a bond. Threads are spun, thoughts and feelings enter a connection. That's Jo and Matthew.

We leave Quillan with the certainty that everything will take its course. We'll come back. We've found a special place and already formed friendships. We just know it. Or perhaps, everything just happens, and we're just puppets in a beautiful game that we must surrender to. *Quillan chooses you* - Jane's words.

November 2023

Quickly out onto the terrace, soak up a little sun. This light, these colours. Impulses that go straight from the eyes to the heart. It's good that I'm still free, not going back to remote work until the day after tomorrow. Tassilo is working downstairs, occasionally his hotspot drops out.

The mountains opposite become shrouded in clouds by noon; I see only a few vultures. Quillan is in winter slumber. I like that. Only at night does the flashing Christmas lights in front of our living room remind me of some life.

The Aude has so little water; we're worried. The rush has become quieter. When we first came here, the level was half a metre higher. And it stays low, getting lower. That's why a rainy day is a good day. Quillan needs the Aude, we need the Aude. It's my elixir; looking at it gives me energy and takes away all stress. My fears that I couldn't bear this noise – completely unfounded.

The tranquility behind the rush. Being with myself and within myself. The best place in the world to find peace within yourself. Closest thing to crazy.

And the best place in the world to figure out: what do I really want, now, for the last big chapter of my life?

Tassilo is making a career, enabling us through his work to have this life. My priorities have realigned. I want to write more. I want more time for peace and more time in nature. Allowing new ideas and seeing what comes out of them. Taking care of household chores without stress, focusing on friends, family. Unpaid care work, well, it's always a matter of money. What solution, what compromise can be found? We've been together for nineteen years now, raised our children into wonderful people, had fantastic family years together. Now they're going their own ways, out of the house, no longer needing care.

Our couple life together is somehow still under construction. Quillan is a first, new step on this path. Are we on the right track? Will there be THE compromise? What might it look like? Am I perhaps just a restless spirit, always wanting to move on? How much time do we give Quillan, might it eventually push us away?

Will there ever be a music stand somewhere, with a song that signals us to move on?

I decide to live in the here and now, to enjoy each day as it is, wherever I may be. Right now, it's Quillan. Jo across the way waves to me. In the words of Keane, this is somewhere only we know.

To be continued . . . .

Jo's Story

Yes, I will marry you, I said, *but I want to have adventures.*

He took me at my word. A year after we married, we found ourselves living and working in the middle of the Kalahari Desert in Botswana. Thirty years later, we're here in the Aude Valley.

Mattie and I met at Reading University in 1989. We had both signed up to the PGCE; a post graduate Drama and English Teacher training course. He'd been working in London for a few years in a television production company, after completing his degree in Performing Arts and travelling around Australia. He had spent that summer cycling through the Picos de Europa in Spain. He was fit, sun-kissed, clever, great fun and the only male on the course. So we soon became good friends, squash partners and took part in the Uni production of Macbeth, in which I murdered him. We quickly realised that there was more to this relationship than just friends and the rest, as they say, is history.

In retrospect it was, therefore, a good decision to do the PGCE. I had just finished my Film and Drama degree at Reading and grappled with the realisation that I was never going to fulfil my long-held dream of being an actor. Despite my best intentions and a certain devotion to the theatre, I had to admit to myself that I wasn't good enough to become a professional. I wouldn't be good enough to support myself and provide security for a possible future family. So, rather reluctantly at first, I decided to stay in familiar Reading where I knew and liked my tutors and start out on the difficult journey of becoming a teacher.

I don't think this career choice was really a surprise to my family. As the eldest of three girls, I had always been bossy and teacherly towards my poor sisters, Sophie and Lucie. Growing up in rural Essex, we had a pretty idyllic childhood. We lived in an Elizabethan thatched cottage with diamond shaped windows, surrounded by corn fields and not much else. Dad — Tony, ran a restaurant in London and only came home at weekends, exhausted. So Mum — Jan, brought the three of us up pretty much on her own. She was (and still is) an incredible Mum. Hard-working, kind, creative, warm, beautiful and good fun. We weren't poor and were always well fed, but there was never any money for luxuries, the latest toys and holidays abroad. None of that mattered much. We were content with our lot and our annual two weeks in Cornwall, where my parents always seemed their happiest and most relaxed.

Mum is a great cook and she set up and ran her own catering company from the cottage. So we would get out from under her busy feet by spending all our days, whatever the weather, outside in the fields, making dens, role playing story book characters, climbing trees, arriving home hungry and filthy. When it was really too wet or cold to play outside, I would set up a classroom in my bedroom and make my compliant siblings spend hours doing sums and spellings. Sophie and Lucie recall with good grace and some amusement how I would shut them in my wardrobe if they were naughty. Thankfully, my adult teaching style has been, or so I am told, much kinder and rather more creative.

Despite being, in the main, a family of dyslexics, I had managed to learn to read quickly and one of my resounding memories of primary school was at the age of ten, being asked by the teacher, Mr Daggert, to teach a small traveller boy to read. Tommy was sweet and smiley and seemed happier to be taught by me than scary Mr Daggert. He was a good student, focused and hard-working and made fast progress. I can still remember that feeling of shared joy when the story he was reading suddenly began to make sense to him. So, yes, I should have known that teaching was to be my future.

From an early age the theatre became a passion. It all started when Mum and Dad took me at about age six to see an amateur production of *My Fair*

Lady by The Dunmow Players. I thought it was the most exciting thing I had ever seen and I loved the tragic beauty of Eliza Doolittle. From that moment I knew I wanted to learn to act, sing and dance. I started having ballet lessons and soon became involved in the annual Dunmow pantomime, a huge community event, directed by my wonderful elderly ballet teacher, Lillian Judges. It became a family affair as Sophie and Lucie soon joined and as Mum was a good dressmaker, she was invited to make many of the costumes. Over the years she must have made hundreds of beautiful costumes of all shapes and sizes on her old sewing machine. I don't know how she did it. Surviving on very little sleep I think. But my sisters and I had so much fun taking part. I worked my way up from being a little robin, to an elf, a fairy, a villager and then the dizzy heights of Principal Girl. I think I gained so much confidence from this experience so that when I got to Secondary school, I was lucky to land some of the best parts in the school productions; Eliza in *My Fair Lady*, Maria in *West Side Story*. My introduction to Shakespeare though, came from our beloved maternal grandmother, who we always called Yog. She had been to RADA and had wanted to act, but soon the Second World War had broken out and she'd married my grandfather Hugh, followed him out to India and sadly never got to do any serious acting.

I remember, aged fourteen, going to see Yog in Suffolk, where she and G Father settled after the war. I told her that I wanted to audition for the part of Helena in the school production of *A Midsummer Night's Dream*. My comprehensive school education had, so far, only been comprehensive up to a point. I had never studied Shakespeare or even seen a Shakespeare play. The language was alien to me and I was struggling with the chosen monologue. I badly needed her help. Yog was delighted and we snuck up to the attic bedroom so no one else could hear us. She began to read Helena's sorrowful lines which bemoan her lack of beauty in comparison to her friend, Hermia. I was transfixed, close to tears. The way Yog read the lines at last made sense and the character sprang from the page. She then patiently guided me through the piece. Yet, as with all good teachers, she encouraged me to establish my own interpretation. I got the part and fell in love with Shakespeare.

Having completed my A Levels, at eighteen, I wanted to follow in Yog's footsteps and go to Drama School. But several excruciating auditions and rejection letters later, it became clear that I needed a different course of action. I decided to take a couple of years out of education while I decided what to do with my life. As it turns out, this was to have been a good decision as they were the only two years in fifty, when I was not in some form of educational establishment. It is a fundamental error of the British system, that teachers are not entitled to sabbaticals as they are in many countries around the world. The teacher drop-out rate might be considerably lower if, after twenty years of service, we were given the opportunity to recharge our batteries.

But enough ranting. Back to the gap years. I had always wanted to learn to ski so, with my French A Level in hand, I went off to work as a waitress in a hotel for the winter season in a ski resort in Crans-Montana, Switzerland. This was great for improving my French as I was the only English speaker in my hotel. But the work was tough and the hours long. I worked the first six weeks, seven days a week without a single day off. I had done a fair bit of waitressing in the past, particularly for my Mum at weddings, but I had to learn Silver Service on the job and keep up with the other two waiters; a young, supercilious French guy and a rather surly, but gorgeous Italian! They were both quite disgusted that I should be working alongside them, when they had both been to Catering College and were far more qualified than me. Fair point. They made my life difficult every day in the kitchen and dining room, shouting at me rather too easily about any small mistake, until they realised that my chatty and pleasant demeanour with the customers resulted in good tips, which I shared with the two of them. That soon shut them up!

I had to be up early for breakfasts, had a short break before lunch duty and then did the evening meals. So the afternoons were my own. This was my opportunity to ski. The mountains were beautiful and inviting, what could possibly go wrong?

I bought some rather well-used but cheap second-hand skis, poles and boots from a hire shop near my hotel. I couldn't afford lessons so I messed around on my own on the nursery slopes for the first week, making little progress and avoiding going up the mountain in the cable car, for fear of not being able to get back down once I'd set off. Then a girl from Cumbria who was working in the hotel next to mine and was an excellent skier, told me to stop being ridiculous. Sharon agreed to accompany me up the mountain and help me ski down. So, gripping a season ski pass and sweating hideously from the too many layers I had thought would be essential at the colder top of the mountain, we climbed into the cable car. My first. The views were stunning, but I don't think my nerves and the feelings of nausea allowed me to really appreciate them on this first journey. Sharon was lovely; friendly, encouraging, an elegant skier. But it was probably one of the scariest moments of my life when she introduced me to a fairly icy, mogaly red run. As I looked down the incredibly steep mountain I wanted to cry. I ended up tumbling my way down, spending much of the run on my bottom. Luckily, I have improved somewhat. I love skiing now but I'm still pretty bad at it and have sustained a number of injuries over the years, more recently resulting in the use of crutches and months of physio on my knee. A ski instructor friend once said; *Jo, you've got a lot of bottle, but no style.* Great, thanks.

There were several young Brits from the same recruitment company as me, working in other hotels in Crans-Sur-Sierre. As a somewhat naïve eighteen-year-old from the countryside (and needing desperately to get away from my rather unpleasant work colleagues and my loneliness), I was delighted to meet up with them in the après ski bars and indulge in the night club scene when work finished around 10 p.m. I went out nearly every night and had a ball. We would dance until 2 or 3 a.m., go back to our hotels and sleep deeply until the rude awakening of our alarms at 6.30 a.m., grabbing the odd hour or so throughout the day to sleep off our excesses of the night! I don't know how I survived on so little sleep for four months. But it was worth it. I had a lot of fun, made some great friends, had a French boyfriend from Toulouse who was a chef at the hotel next to mine, learnt to ski, improved my French and even went home with some savings.

Sadly, not long after my return, my parents separated and then divorced. It was a really difficult time for Mum who was devastated. It was hard on

Sophie and Lucie too as they were still at home and did their best to support her. I was living in London with my boyfriend but went back to Essex when I could. I drifted from job to job, feeling a bit lost. Most memorably I worked in the food hall at Harrods, designing hampers — that was a great job; worked on a bar at the Royal Festival Hall and then did a six month secretarial course which Mum paid for and persuaded me to do. I think she was beginning to despair that I would ever do anything useful with my life. But having completed my shorthand and typing course and signed up with an employment agency, I proved to be a useless secretary. Unfortunately, my family dyslexia reared its head when I discovered that all my shorthand was back to front and I couldn't read back and accurately type up any letters the bosses dictated to me. None of the jobs lasted very long. I hated being stuck in an office anyway and soon realised that I was ready to get back to studying. I wanted to taste University life.

My two gap years had not been a complete cultural void. I would raid the Shaftesbury Avenue bookshops, filling bags with well thumbed plays, devouring them on my many train journeys to and from work. I would try to see the latest plays at the National Theatre and kept an eye out for experimental fringe productions that I could afford and travel to easily.

So, I thought, why not combine my love of drama, the theatre, film and books in a Combined degree in Film and Drama with Modern English Literature. Thus began what turned out to be four years at the University of Reading. Happy, carefree, creative years. And it was here that my love of travel was cemented by an extraordinary trip when I met my dear friend and fellow student Buffy. We backpacked round India and Nepal for a month in the Easter of 1987. A trek in the Himalayas, as well as visits to the Taj Mahal, the River Ganges at Varanasi, Jaipur and Kathmandu would ensure a life long connection with India. I have been three times now and long to go back. But the trip was to have even greater significance for Buffy when we met charming Australian traveller Graeme. A few years later they married and settled in Oz, soon giving birth to my godson Fred, followed closely by four more kids, sharing life together on a farm in the Wimmera region of western Victoria. Buffy and Graeme are testament to how travel really can shape your future.

During my second year at University Mum met Bob, a gentle giant of a man who was to play a very important part in all our lives. We adored him. He was such a positive, happy man with a great belly laugh. He was so supportive of everything we did and always interested to hear our stories, especially as he had no children of his own. He adored Mum, taking her away on exotic holidays, playing bridge together with friends, eating out and having a social life. A complete change for Mum. Bob even walked me down the aisle at my wedding, but not before he'd persuaded my brother-in-law, Jeffrey, who was driving us to the church, to drive around the block a couple of times while he questioned me about whether I was sure I wanted to go ahead with it! He didn't believe in marriage and although we always called him our Stepfather, he and Mum never actually married. He was twenty years older than Mum and very sadly died on Bonfire Night in 2021 aged a hundred. A few days before he died he finally asked Mum to marry him, the old devil! She said it was too late. We miss him.

I started to see my Dad again after ten long years of no contact and the realisation as an adult that marriage and relationships can be complicated. We chat on the phone sometimes and I enjoy going to see him when I can. He always loved seeing me in plays and he and Mel managed to get up to Lincolnshire a couple of times when I was performing in local theatres there. But I know it disappointed him that I never made it in professional theatre.

In some ways, being a Drama teacher fulfilled that desire to stay close to the theatre, plays and play-making. After a teaching baptism of fire in a tough London school, two years teaching in Africa, then North Yorkshire, I spent twenty years teaching drama and English in Lincolnshire, latterly becoming a Visiting Lecturer in Drama Teaching at Lincoln University. Teaching is a tough gig and every day brings new challenges. But I'm glad I chose this career. In the main, it has been fulfilling and varied. Never a dull moment. I worked with incredibly talented and dedicated colleagues. Some became good friends and keep in touch. Most notably, Parissa, Garrath and Deb, all of whom, I am happy to say, have been to visit us here in France several times.

For some of those years Mattie and I worked together running the Drama department, overseeing GCSE and A Level performance work, directing the school productions and taking students on trips to theatres in London, Leeds, Sheffield, Bradford and, of course, Stratford-Upon-Avon. These experiences gave me some very happy memories with wonderful students who were passionate about the theatre. Several of them have become successful actors or playwrights, or drama teachers themselves. It's always a pleasure to hear from them, support their work and catch up over dinner.

After the first twenty years in the job, although I still liked what I was doing, I felt the need for change. I decided that I was becoming too old to retrain in a new career so in addition to teaching Drama and English, I also set up a GCSE Dance course and ran a Fencing club. Both new challenges, but very enjoyable and, to some degree, helped to keep me fit.

As for Mattie, when he applied for the teaching job at the grammar school where I was Head of Drama, he had been asked if he would take on the responsibility of running the school sailing club. He admitted that he'd never sailed before but would be willing to learn. Never being one to do things by halves, he signed up for every sailing course he could find, travelling all over the country, Turkey and the Greek Islands, soon becoming incredibly proficient. He ended up running not only the school sailing club, but the local district sailing association. Some of his students went on to compete at national and international level and sailing became a big part of his life.

In order to get to spend more time with him, I decided to train for my Power Boat qualification, gained my PB2 licence and soon began to help out at the club. It was so much fun, especially on a warm evening in the Summer term; zooming about the lake, avoiding the swans to set the sailing course, hoiking children into the boat if they were struggling. We also ran sailing courses in the summer holidays and my niece Lola, nephews Harvey, Otto and Theo, my cousin's son Cameron and my good friend Bib's daughter Florence, used to come and camp in our garden and join us to learn to sail. It was such a privilege spending time with them and great for the cousins to get together, especially when we all sat down for dinner to chew over the water adventures of the day.

I think that my parents being in the hospitality business, and having a Mum who is a great cook, has given me a love of good food and sharing meals that I especially appreciate here in France. I am a useless cook and feel very lucky to have married a man who is so at home in the kitchen, always creating new and delicious dishes and now relishing the markets and fresh locally grown produce so readily available here in our part of the South of France. Every Wednesday and Saturday he comes back from the market with an array of cheeses, including the best goat's cheese we've ever tasted; local honey, olives, vegetables of all shapes, sweet tasting fruits and fresh free range eggs. Even living in Africa, in the desert, eight hours away from the nearest city, his culinary exploits didn't disappoint. Our first year in Botswana he had asked me, as there were no restaurants in the village, what I would like him to cook for my birthday. I joked flippantly that I could murder a cheese soufflé. So he did indeed cook me the most spectacular and scrumptious cheese soufflé; perhaps the only one ever cooked in the Kalahari!

We had left the comfort of our beautiful garden flat in Putney, very sensibly letting it to Sophie and Jeff, in whose capable DIY hands it was in much better shape when we returned. Our two years in Botswana were extraordinary and we've been dining out on the stories of our adventures ever since! During the last thirty years I'm sure our poor friends have had to endure these tales several times over, but have politely resisted revealing the repetitions as they can see how much pleasure we find in the retelling and reliving.

We arrived in the capital city Gaborone in August 1992. The Overseas Development Agency placed all one hundred of us English and Irish teachers in the Sheraton Hotel for two weeks acclimatisation, local language learning and cultural awareness classes. The classes were great and the hotel with its air conditioning, swimming pool and huge buffets, was fantastically luxurious but not the Africa we had imagined. However, meeting other teachers and creating a support network for each other for the years ahead would prove to be invaluable. Some of us had already spent a long training weekend together a couple of months before at Farnham Castle and it was here that we met our dear friends from Somerset, Kate and Greg. They were posted to a school in a village not far from the capital. Kate was an Art teacher and her accompanying husband Greg managed to find work at a college teaching car mechanics. We were to spend many happy weekends and holidays in their company during our time in Botswana and remain good friends to this day.

Of all the teachers in the group of one hundred, we were the only ones to request a rural school posting. This meant that we were sent to the most isolated government school, right in the middle of Botswana; a small town, Kang in the Kalahari Desert. In those days it took eight hours on a sandy track to reach it from the capital. We politely declined an offer of a lift on the back of a government flatbed truck that was dropping teachers all over the country. We saw the huge iron cooking pots and sacks of food being loaded onto the back and asked how long the journey would take. We were told the truck was going north first before heading out into the desert so would get to Kang in about two weeks! Although this might have been an interesting experience, meeting other Batswana colleagues and sleeping under the stars around a camp fire, we reasoned that it was going to be essential to have a car out there. So we waved the truck off and Mattie went in search of a truck of our own. But first he needed to secure a loan from the bank.

Early the next morning he jumped onto an empty bus from outside the hotel, headed to the banking quarter of the Capital. The bus soon filled up along the way with people going to work. Finally, after a very hot and rather uncomfortable journey, M reached his destination. As he was walking away from his stop, he heard shouting. He turned back towards the bus and the driver was leaning out of the door, waving something in the air:

White man, white man, you've forgotten your wallet.

It had fallen out of his shorts pocket and the kind passenger next to him had handed it in. This was a great introduction to, in our experience, the lovely people of Botswana.

However, administration and bureaucracy was a different matter. For three days in a row Matthew sat in the reception area of Barclays in Gaborone, waiting to talk to the Bank Manager. Eventually, when it was obvious that he was serious and not going to give up, he was ushered into a large office. He was greeted with a firm handshake by a broad, middle aged African man in a suit, who listened carefully to the story of our remote posting. He agreed that a truck was a necessity out there but that it had to be a reliable one, thereby requiring a larger loan than we had anticipated. He asked Matthew if he had a bank in England. M provided some paperwork. The Bank Manager picked up his phone and dialled the UK bank:

Hello Madame, I'm telephoning from Barclays Bank in Botswana .....
Oh, one of our customers, a Mr O'Neill recently went to work in Botswana.
Yes! Can you vouch for him being a reliable customer Madame?
Oh certainly Sir.

Such was the banking service of old and we were granted our loan. But not before the Bank Manager had grabbed his own car keys and asked M to follow him to the car park. He then drove him round to several car dealers before finding the car that he was prepared to loan us the money for; a gleaming, dark green Toyota Hilux that was registered near Kang. That way it would less likely be stolen, he assured us.

So another lesson learned. Patience and courtesy go a long way in Africa.

The next day, with a mixture of excitement and trepidation, we said goodbye to the staff at the Sheraton who for two weeks had made us feel so welcome and to Kate and Greg, with a promise to come back and stay with them at their school the following month.

The journey was like no other we had ever taken. The tarmac road out of Gaborone soon turned into a sand track, which took some getting used to as a driver (and passenger). The truck would so easily slide on the uneven surface. Amongst the many camel thorn trees dotted about the desert we soon spotted ostriches. These huge, comic birds can move incredibly fast and love to run alongside cars or suddenly appear in front of you, a whole family crossing the track ahead, so we were on high alert to give plenty of time for braking on the sandy surface.

After eight hours of heat and dust, as the sun was setting, we finally arrived in Kang to begin a new chapter in our lives. On the outskirts of the town were many rondavels: beautiful, round, thatched huts adorned with colourful patterns, where women crouched over cast iron pots, stirring the stews to feed their families. The centre of the town was more commercial with small shops, bars, a wholesale business and Matcha Community College, where we would live and work for the next two years.

On arrival we were greeted by the Headteacher, Mr Mokete, a tall, imposing Batswana of around forty, who immediately showed us to our house and left us to settle in. We were astonished to find a very pleasant three bedroomed house with a veranda, large sitting room, kitchen and shower room with a loo and sink. It was all quite basic but more than adequate for our needs. The solar panels on the roof that were supposed to bring us hot water never worked, but we got used to cold showers and were grateful for any water at all. The women and children in the village had to walk a mile to collect theirs from the borehole, carrying it home on their heads in the desert heat.

Over the weeks that followed I enjoyed spending time making the house more homely. I bought throws, cushions, candles and locally made ornaments from the San, Bushmen. I experimented with batiks for the walls and purchased an old Singer sewing machine from Gaborone on one of our trips back to stay with Kate and Greg and stock up on supplies. With my new trusty machine I made curtains for all the rooms from an array of brightly coloured African fabrics. I attempted to make a patchwork out of all the remnants. It was never finished.

We also got to know our neighbours, the Zambian Deputy Head, his beautiful wife and their three small children. They were great neighbours; very kind to us and the children were sweet and always smiling and curious about us, I remember. We were employed to teach the Cambridge O Level English Language and Literature courses, which were a little old fashioned by this point but were still being offered overseas and marked by examiners in the UK. It seemed somewhat unfair and rather ironic that our children from the Kalahari had to answer questions about sailing and water activities in the exam. But we loved the teaching as the children highly valued education, were so incredibly keen to learn, charming and good fun.

In addition to our English teaching responsibilities, we also taught some P.E. and Computer Studies. Yes, believe it or not there were ten Apple Mac computers kept in an air conditioned room in this school in the middle of the Kalahari. Mattie was great at it. I think the students taught me more about computers than I could teach them. But I did help them to touch type — one of the few skills I had learnt at secretarial college. I also set up a modern dance club at the request of the thirty girls who keenly attended every week. It was fabulous as we had a lot of laughs and were asked to perform at a local festival. They taught me some of their traditional dance routines too.

The majority of the students wanted to secure a different existence from the tough rural lives of their parents and grandparents. They mostly wanted to go to University and then live and work in the city. I sincerely hope that we helped them towards bright and fulfilling futures.

Some evenings and weekends, if we weren't travelling back to Gaborone to see Kate and Greg or camping in the bush, we would spend time with our local friends, particularly a wonderful young couple and their baby who had left South Africa to set up a wholesale business in Kang. The generosity, warmth and friendship of Elmarie and Léan and their beautiful house and garden was like an oasis in the desert. One of the benefits of social media is that despite not having seen them for over thirty years, we have remained friends. We would love to see them again one day and offer them our hospitality.

Having twenty-six weeks holiday over the two years there meant plenty of time to explore the rest of Botswana and surrounding countries. One of the most beautiful places to camp and watch the extraordinary array of birds and animals was the Okavango Delta in the north of Botswana. It is such a unique place and still so relatively wild and unspoilt. You really can't beat seeing elephants, giraffe, lions, leopards, hyenas, hippos, crocs, baboons and wild dogs in their natural environment. We loved it and went as often as we could, camping at Third Bridge which had a very small concrete block with a loo and shower and nothing else there. Not even fences separating you from the animals, thankfully. We would often be the only people camping there and frequently heard hyenas sniffing round the tent at night, the loud roaring of lions in the distance, the snapping of branches or the swaying of the tent itself as elephants squeezed past us, delicately stepping over guy ropes. We would often find Lion spore around the tent in the morning. We became used to sharing the place with the animals and were respectful of their territory and their power. But it frightened the life out of our visiting family and friends.

We were also aware, however, that we were so close to many other extraordinary countries and that we should make the most of our short time living in Africa to travel more widely. The highlight of our travel adventures was our first Christmas holiday when we drove in convoy with Kate and Greg to stay with Kate's uncle in Nairobi. We camped along the way, staying on the banks of the Zambezi river in Zambia and on the shores of Lake Malawi, as well as a few nights of relative luxury in small hotels in Zimbabwe and Tanzania.

One of my everlasting memories of the trip happened after several beers in a bar in Zambia. On arrival the owner said we were welcome to pitch our tents on the banks of the Zambezi. After a joyous evening of good food, cold beers and games of cards, we tumbled into our tents. Unfortunately the beers got the better of me and after a few hours I woke up desperate to pee. I unzipped the tent and was just about to step out when, a few feet away, the yellow moonlight revealed the riverbank covered in about fifty huge sleeping crocodiles. Needless to say I did not pee outside but, to Mattie's disgust, squatted down on the grass in the tent porch! By morning the crocs had all slithered back into the water and disappeared. Swimming was definitely not an option for us that morning.

But swimming in Lake Malawi a couple of days later was lovely and refreshing in the heat, although we had to be very careful to avoid the hippos, the animal responsible for more deaths than any other in Africa. We were lucky not to encounter them and enjoy this huge swathe of water that covers much of the country. I have mostly fond memories of our short time in Malawi, especially at one point feeling peckish and stopping to pick my favourite fruit, a ripe, juicy mango from a tree on the side of the road belonging to no one in particular.

However, there was a bad memory. Too many hours and days driving had taken its toll on M and he developed excruciating back pain. So I insisted on driving for what turned out to be probably the worst drive of my life. It was dusk and we were a couple of hours away from the border with Tanzania. The heavens opened and the narrow track through the hills became a slippery mud bath. We were losing daylight and at points there was a sheer drop to one side. Gripping the steering wheel, I followed Kate and Greg's tracks, slowly manoeuvring the truck through treacherous terrain with the rain lashing down and the windscreen wipers smacking back and forth. It required an inordinate amount of concentration and perseverance and seemed to go on forever. On finally crossing into Tanzania in the dark, I was so relieved that I burst into tears. That night we stayed in the relative luxury of a small, family run hotel and recuperated, ready for the next hurdle.

I loved Tanzania. My most vivid memory was driving into the sunset towards majestic Mount Kilimanjaro, red clothed Masai dotting the slopes. Suddenly a giraffe stepped in front of us, slowly, gracefully crossing the road. She was beautiful, elegant, owning the road and the place. I will never forget her and our short time in Tanzania.

Getting across the border into Kenya was not so elegant. The authorities wanted us to pay a huge amount of money to effectively import our cars. It took many hours and a few bribes to convince the border authorities that we were only holidaying in Kenya for a few days.

Finally we arrived in Nairobi nine days after setting off from Botswana. Kate's uncle and his partner gave us such a good welcome. It was fun exploring the city a bit and buying our Christmas presents for everyone and each other. We had a very jolly Christmas of good food, great company, card games and comfortable beds. Then, five days later, we set off again for the long journey home.

Kate and Greg went to stay in a Safari Lodge for a few days, a Christmas present from her uncle, so we headed off to do some walking in the foothills of Mount Kenya. A stunning place to hike. We then crossed back into Tanzania (much more uneventfully this time) and headed to the Ngorongoro Crater, a volcanic conservation area in Northern Tanzania where you can see a fantastic number of different species of birds and animals roaming freely but in a relatively small area.

One of the other highlights of the trip back was going to the beautiful island of Zanzibar, a ferry ride from Dar es Salaam. We loved its maize of narrow streets in the old stone town, the wonderful Arabic architecture and extraordinary huge doors, delicious street food, long sandy beaches and crystal clear waters. We stayed at Africa House Hotel, remarkable for the sunsets over the ocean, viewed from the roof terrace. We saw in the New Year at a reggae party, meeting up by chance with old friends from London and dancing until four in the morning. Such an incredible island and good memories made.

Over our two years in Africa we did several other trips in our faithful truck, often with family or friends visiting from the UK. Both Sophie and Lucie and their partners visited and even my dear Mum. None of these adventures were quite as remarkable for them as the long journey to Kenya had been for us, but were nevertheless interesting and exciting, including white water rafting the rapids at the base of Victoria Falls, tracking lions not far from Kang, having a clan of cackling hyenas running around our tents and sharing a shower with a thirsty elephant in Savuti. My wonderful sisters and Mum were so brave! We enjoyed holidays with visiting friends to Zimbabwe, Namibia and South Africa. And on our flight home to the UK managed to stop off back in Zanzibar and the fabulous Kenyan Island of Lamu. Two years we will never forget.

Back in the UK we soon decided that we wanted to start a family and that London was not where we wanted to be, or more to the point, could afford to be. So we then went to live and work on the gorgeous North Yorkshire coast where I gave birth to our first child in 1996.

Our beautiful Daisy was an absolute delight and changed our lives forever. Her natural warmth and joy for life have continued into adulthood. She has taken up the mantle of our family tradition by becoming a teacher of A Level Photography at a college and also an Assistant Sailing Instructor. I had the pleasure of teaching her on my dance GCSE course at school and she was astonishing for her choreographic skills, gaining full marks for all her dances in her exam. She is also very musical and for a time lead the school orchestra as first violin. Daisy never ceases to amaze me at how capable she is, yet always modest and gracious, kind and considerate of others. And unlike her mother, is a good cook too! She was recently asked by the college to teach A Level History of Art as they were a teacher short. Daisy agreed to take on the challenge and saved the course from closure. She and I had a day in London together a few months after she started teaching the course. It was enlightening to study some of the paintings together in the National Gallery with her knowledge and gentle guidance. I know she is a great teacher and will inspire many young people over the coming years. I love staying with Daisy, her partner Neil and their step-daughter Bonnie in Brighton as they always make me so welcome, spoiling me by taking me to my first ever football match, enjoying live music together, games of Poker at the local pub, introducing me to their friends and making me feel young again!

Twenty-two months after Daisy was born, her wonderful sister Holly came into our lives, completing our little family. Holly was feisty and fun, determined to keep up with her older sister. She has always been hard-working and academic, creative and successful at everything she does and continues to be such great company in adulthood. She is an excellent netball player and has recently taken up running, determined to improve on her times week by week. She also shares her Dad's passion for cycling. She is my film and shopping buddy and we both love singing and harmonising together in the car or in the kitchen, just as Mum and I did when I was a kid! Holly is an accomplished Grade 8 singer and is often asked to sing solos at family weddings and funerals. But it is being part of a communal choir that she really enjoys. Holly and her husband Simon are passionate animal lovers and now successfully follow a vegan diet. A few years ago Simon famously saved a chicken by taking it from a battery farm, tucking it under his jacket and cycling home with it — a story mentioned in several of the speeches at their fabulous wedding on a sunny day in July 2022. Hol and Simon take us on beautiful hikes every time we visit them in Lancashire where they've made their happy home. Both our daughters now love to go hiking, despite being reluctantly dragged along with us when they were young.

Becoming a Mum definitely had its challenges, especially as the girls were so close in age. As most people who have taken the parental journey would agree, I think you spend years trying to function on very little sleep, never having enough money and trying desperately to remain professional in your job — trying not to be angry or late when you have sick, egg or poo on your clothes. Trying to be patient with childish frustrations and tantrums, giving advice and guidance but not suffocating and stifling individuality. There's no rehearsals, so we make it up as we go along and hope we get it right. I can't imagine how tough it must be for single parents. I was privileged to have the constant support, patience and partnership of Mattie. He's a great Dad.

As I write, our daughters are both pregnant with their first children, due a few days apart! I wonder what joys motherhood will bring them. I can't wait to be a grandmother.

Parenthood definitely brought us adventures. In 2015 the girls and I were given backstage tickets for Glastonbury, thanks to our dear friend Tec. (Mattie, never a fan of crowds, said he preferred to watch it all on TV). We spent two incredible days seeing some great bands, catching up with Lucie and her family, spending time with Tec when he could take time away from his band and camping in relative luxury. I had been to Glastonbury with friends seven years before this, but there was something very special about sharing the experience with Daisy and Holly. Thanks to Tec we had similar experiences at V Fest for several years running too, where his wife — Daisy's godmother — my gorgeous school friend Bib and I once looked on as our girls: Florence, Daisy and Holly, chatted with Ed Sheeran back stage.

Mattie and I were determined to introduce the girls to a wider world outside of Lincolnshire and the UK, so travel was a very important part of their growing up. We were lucky to have the school holidays all together. Camping trips to Ireland and France were always fun. And a few days in Paris when the queue for the Eiffel Tower lift was too long and the girls ran all the way up the 674 steps to the second floor. And we spent many memorable summers staying with our lovely friends, the Daltons, in the Isles of Scilly; idyllic trips in Jim's boat, sailing to uninhabited islands, swimming with seals, fishing and crabbing, eating great food — usually cooked by Sarah, sometimes caught by us; card and board games when it was wet, playing cricket on the white sandy beaches or just relaxing in the sun with a good book. The two families got on so well together and we were always grateful to be invited back each year for many summers.

Then in the summer of 2008, my Uncle James invited the four of us to Vancouver for the trip of a lifetime. After he and my aunt Peggie welcomed us at their fabulous home for several days and introduced us to the delights of Vancouver, he organised for us to go on the Rocky Mountaineer train from Vancouver to Banff through the stunning Rockies. Definitely one of the best train rides in the world. During our month in Canada my uncle was incredibly generous and ensured that we stayed in some fabulous hotels — a real first for Daisy and Holly, most notably on the shores of the turquoise waters of Lake Louise and in Victoria on Vancouver Island. Highlights on the island included staying in a luxury apartment on the beach in Tofino, watching the antics of magnificent hump back whales, staying with James, Peggie and my cousin Becca at a holiday home in Qualicum and hiking and wild camping at a glacial lake with bears!

Our childhood holidays in Cornwall had been about reconnecting with family too. A time to catch up with my paternal grandfather and his tiny wife Taptie, who lived near St Austell. We stayed in my Great Aunt and Uncle's fabulous holiday home in Trenarren, a long walk down the narrow, winding path from the cliff top with all our belongings to the large house, an old fish factory and the beach and jetty at the bottom. A time to enjoy the stunning Cornish coast; bathing and boating in Dad's boat, fishing for mackerel — ingeniously smoked by Mum in her ersatz biscuit tin on sawdust and a neatly fitting grill; catching spider crabs and the occasional lobster in our lobster pots; walking the coastal path, reading, relaxing and having fun with my aunt and uncle, Caroline and Nigel and cousins Amanda and Nicola who joined us most summers. Idyllic childhood memories where it was always sunny. I know that's not the reality. There was plenty of rain but not in my head. I have always greatly valued these experiences. Spending time with loving extended family is not just about weddings and funerals.

So we continued this holiday tradition — our travels with the girls and my sisters and their families taking us to beautiful, remote villas in Italy and France, skiing in Andorra and renting a cottage in West Wales with Mum. Likewise we have shared magical Christmases here in France with Matthew's sister Maria and her husband Conor and their children; our nieces Saoirse and Aiobhe and nephew Johnjo, introducing them to snails, quails eggs, oysters and skiing! We have spent happy times with them at their holiday house on the coast in Connemara, Ireland too, catching up with Auntie Helen and Holly's Godfather Gerry over raucous games of the O'Neill family card game 110. We're so lucky to have such a close, supportive and loving family.

Over the years we also explored Portugal, Spain, Mallorca, Morocco, Tunisia, The Gambia, Egypt and India. I'm delighted that the girls both love to travel and together with their partners Neil and Simon and friends, take off to interesting parts of the world.

People often ask me which age of my children I enjoyed the most. I always find it hard to answer that question. I have loved and continue to love each stage. I can honestly say that becoming a Mum was the best thing I ever did and would do it all over again, if only I could! We are incredibly proud of them both, not because of their considerable achievements (they both have First Class degrees and good jobs), but because of the compassionate, hard-working, fun, gracious people they have become. I hope they both find as much joy in motherhood as I do.

They both like to visit us in Quillan, but it was Holly who found our lovely southern French market town.

My experiences of France had started as a naïve twelve year old, staying with a French family near Montpellier for two weeks every year for four summers. I really loved my time with my French friend Christine and her family and despite being given sheep's brains for my first meal, my love affair with France was well and truly ignited. I also did some camping in France with my parents and a boyfriend in my late teens when Dad got fed up with the wet holidays in Cornwall and wanted to find the sun.

So I realised quite early on in life that one day I would like to live in France or retire here. As ever, Mattie was very amenable to helping me follow my dreams and for several summer holidays from 2014 to 2016, once Daisy and Holly decided they would like to go off on holiday with their boyfriends, he and I would take off on the motorbike and explore different areas in the hope of finding somewhere in France that we might call home sometime in the future.

The following year in 2017 the dream was to turn into reality. Mattie came up with a brainwave. He suggested that we sell the family home in Lincolnshire now that both our girls had left and we were rattling around in it, being reminded daily of their absence; pay off the mortgage, rent a cottage and buy a holiday home in France. That way we could ease ourselves gently into the new language, culture and life style by going there every school holiday. Fabulous idea! So, after nineteen years of living in our Victorian family home in the market town of Horncastle, we sold up and moved to a pretty rental cottage in Lincoln where we were both working. The search for a property in France then began in earnest.

Daisy had won a photography competition, following a family holiday in Africa. The prize was a week's holiday for two in an eco lodge in The Gambia. As I had encouraged her to enter the competition in the first place, she kindly insisted on me accompanying her. And so that Easter we headed off with Bib and Florence for a week of sun, sea and bird watching.

Meanwhile, Matthew and Holly decided to come to France and look at houses. After our motorbike trips we had narrowed down our search to the Aude in the Languedoc Roussillon region. So they based themselves in the beautiful Medieval city of Carcassonne and began their hunt. On the final day, after several viewings of houses in villages that didn't excite them, they came to Quillan. They had a delicious lunch in the main square, La Place de La Rèpublique, overlooking the river Aude and Holly said *This is where you and Mum should live.*

So a few weeks later, in May half term, Mattie and I flew to Carcassonne, hired a car and booked into a hotel in Quillan. I immediately fell in love with this picturesque little town on the river, nestled in the foothills of the Pyrenees with its twice weekly markets, bakeries, cafés, restaurants, music events, theatre, cinema and swimming lake. We loved the opportunities for great walks and cycling in the mountains, the dramatic gorges, the Cathar castles, water sports, the nearby ski resorts, the coast an hour away and the Spanish border just a two hour drive. And so much sunshine. We looked at two houses and third time lucky found our French home on the banks of the river.

One of the first people we talked to was Mischa, who has her own story here to tell. She came over to us as we were sitting in Le Palace brasserie pondering an offer for the house. She reassured us that Quillan was a great place to live and told us not to wait too long as houses rarely come up for sale on the river. She was so right. Thank you Mischa. Our minds were made up and we bought our wonderful house.

It wasn't anything like I'd imagined my French house would be. In my mind we would buy a beautiful old wisteria-covered stone cottage on the outskirts of a picturesque mountain village, with wild rocky land and meadow, cypress trees offering shade and perhaps a pool for cooling off on those hot hot summer days. But instead we bought an old three storey town house with two terraces going down to the fast flowing river. It has very high ceilings, huge vertical beams running all the way through four floors and big rooms with large windows throwing light front and back. We love the space it offers us, especially when the house is brimming with visitors. There's room for everyone. And the river is such a beautiful presence — its roaring, ever-changing ebb and flow home to trout and heron; comedic ducks teaching ducklings to swim the rapids; mink with furry babies exploring the rocky pools; swifts, swallows and *libellules* (dragonflies) swooping down to drink in the summer months. A place of peace and contemplation.

After three years of living here in the holidays and feeling distraught every time we had to lock up and leave our French life, we made a big decision. We were becoming so disillusioned with the UK following the catastrophic Brexit decision, the corrupt government, the rainy grey days and exhaustion after over thirty years of teaching. One night, back in the UK, over a bottle of delicious French red wine M said, *I've been thinking about this for the last two days and I think we should give up our teaching jobs and go and live full time in France.* I was of course delighted to agree!

So we did it. Despite loving my work as Head of English in a Hospital Special School for the last six years of my teaching career, and M running a team of teachers for the Home Tuition Service, we handed in our notices, bought a Luton van to transport the remaining contents of the cottage and moved to France. And we have never regretted it for a moment. M still teaches online to students in the UK in care or with special educational needs. And in the summer he does GCSE English Language exam marking.

I edit and proofread novels, completing ten in the last three years. I also host young and adult French students, often from the north who come and stay with us for a week or two for English lessons, to enjoy Matthew's cooking and explore our region. I get paid to go sightseeing!

This work has brought many positive experiences, but some more memorable than others. One of my students — Nat, a beautiful, black fourteen year old girl from Paris who had stayed with us for two weeks in August 2021, contacted us in the December and asked if her family could come and stay on their way to a holiday in Spain. So two days before Christmas, with the help of Daisy and Neil, we hosted Nat, her Mum and Dad, and her three siblings. It was wonderful and after dinner Daisy and I took Nat and her two older siblings to Melissa's dance class.

Similarly, the following year Stéphane came from the aerospace industry for an intense week of language immersion. He, Matthew and I hit it off immediately, especially when he collected his guitar from his room after dinner one night and we sang songs together until the small hours. He came back six months later with his lovely wife Christelle and their two charming adult daughters as our guests for the weekend.

The highlight in 2022 was being asked to host a group of twenty students from the University of Bordeaux. I organised their accommodation in three houses, including ours. Their lessons were taught in two rotating groups: ten upstairs in our large sitting room with Mattie and ten downstairs with me as I was on crutches following a ski accident! The whole group had all their meals with us on two long trestle tables in our large kitchen, which was a lot of fun and loud chatter, but hard work. Mattie and I did the breakfast each morning, getting up very early to lay tables and get fresh baguettes and croissants from the bakery. He cooked about thirty eggs every day in various guises. Then it all had to be cleared away so we could start the lessons. We made these fun as well as informative, using our drama teaching skills to play games, role play and encourage the students to speak English and interact with one another for the whole week. They said they loved our way of teaching as it was so much more creative and enjoyable than the French education system had ever offered them. Most of them had never done any drama at school and thought they would struggle with it, but on the contrary, they quickly engaged with our teaching style, had fun and grew in confidence.

Our fabulous neighbours Bruno and Gary made fresh, tasty soups every day for lunch, which Bruno brought over to warm up while we were finishing the morning lessons. The last twenty minutes of the morning programme each day was punishing for the students, and for us, as the smell of delicious soups wafted into our teaching spaces, making us famished. For the afternoons I had to organise a range of activities. This was quite tricky as it was February, a time when much of rural France simply closes down. However, I arranged walks in the mountains, a trip to the Medieval city of Carcassonne, a music concert, board games and quizzes. As I was unable to go on the outdoor trips, I asked another of our neighbours Peter, if he would accompany Mattie and be my legs! Not only did he agree to that, but he came and helped every lunchtime and evening with the logistics of the meals. His help was invaluable. We are lucky to have such great neighbours who have become good friends.

I knew that it would be impossible for us to cook all the evening meals as well as teaching and providing activities, so I secured the help of local friends, most of whom have told their stories here. They took it in turns to bring over their delicious dishes each day, including a vegetarian option and most joined us for dinner, enjoying getting to know the students. It all worked out well. The students were delightful and such good company and the University was grateful for all our efforts.

In September of that year we were invited to their graduation ceremony in Bordeaux. The University was offering to pay for our train fairs and three nights in a hotel in the city. How wonderful! Two days before we were due to leave, I received an email from their course tutor asking if I would give a speech at the ceremony about their English language learning experience. There's no such thing as a free lunch, so of course, I agreed. I wrote my speech, translated it into French, had it checked for embarrassing mistranslations by a French friend and we headed off. On arrival at the University, to my horror, it turned out that I was the *only* guest speaker at the ceremony and as my name was called and a microphone was thrust into my hands, I did my best to deliver my speech to the students, their parents and the University staff with as much confidence and as little English accent as I could muster.

Afterwards we were treated to a drinks party of fabulous Bordeaux wine and food. It was great to catch up with the students again and meet their parents. We then had the rest of the weekend to explore the city. What an experience! What a privilege.

I can honestly say that the only thing I miss from the UK is my family and old friends. Sometimes I miss Daisy and Holly terribly. The imminent arrival of our two grandchildren is an incredibly exciting next chapter in our lives. I know that we will travel back to the UK several times a year to see them and help out as and when. And they will come out here to stay with us during some of the holidays. But at the same time I keep telling myself that they have their own lives now and need the freedom to forge their own paths.

I miss my Mum and sisters too, but they like to visit often and we keep in touch almost daily on social media. Luckily for me, Mum and her lovely partner Mike, Lucie, Daisy and Neil all live in East Sussex now, which makes visiting them much easier. Mum and Mike now live on a little farm and make us very welcome there several times a year, Mike stoically putting up with huge numbers of family descending on them and Mum seemingly effortlessly feeding us all. Sophie, Lucie and I also try to holiday together in Europe every June, which is always a right giggle. And Mum and her friend B come to stay in early summer to enjoy some exploring, crafting and wine tasting.

Last year M and I were delighted when M's brother Liam and his partner Susan decided to come and live here in Quillan. It feels good to have family just down the road and it means my sister-in-law Maria comes over more often with her family to visit both her brothers. Always a good time when the Irish all get together!

Many of our old friends come to visit too and it's great catching up with them and hearing the gossip from our old life. Not everything is perfect here, it never is. As others have mentioned, the bureaucracy here is difficult to navigate, especially with the language barriers and post Brexit. Driving here is terrible as people tailgate all the time. And I would like to get to know more local French speakers. But that takes time and more effort I guess.

Luckily I have made fabulous new friends here, originating from all over the world who, like me, enjoy hiking these stunning foothills; camping, cycling, skiing; swimming in our local lake and drying off on the big stone chairs; driving to the coast for seafood and swims at Collioure; exploring our region of Cathar castles and dramatic gorges; going to concerts and art exhibitions; pottering about in *brocantes*; savouring French food and drinking blanquette!

For now, life here in Quillan is truly wonderful.

Acknowledgements

Huge thanks to Tina, Melissa, Paulita, Nicky, Mischa, Sue, Michelle, Christine and Minna for joining me on this writing journey. Your creative minds, friendship, encouragement, patience and good company have seen this project through to the end. It has been a blast!

Thank you Daisy O'Neill and Holly Morton for being the best daughters anyone could ask for. And for reading the first draft of my story and giving invaluable advice. I love you to the moon and back. And thank you Neil Heard-White, Bonnie Chung and Simon Morton for loving them too. What great adventures you all have ahead of you.

Thanks to Sophie Stericker and Lucie Stericker for being the best sisters in the world. I look forward to reading your messages every morning when I wake up and to us continuing our annual sister holiday. Your suggestions about omissions after reading my first draft were great. Thank you Soph for your style ideas and a big thank you Lu for your fabulous book cover design. There's a reason you're an award winning designer.

Thank you to my brother-in-law Jeffery Steventon for hosting us, feeding us and putting on a brave face every time we come to London!

Thank you Jan Stericker for being such a fabulous Mumma and creating a warm and welcoming base for us all to flock to. Your support for everything we do is unstinting and I love your visits, our crafting and our road trips. I hope I have as much energy as you when I'm older. You are an inspiration. Thank you Mike Railton for loving her, welcoming us into your life and putting up with us when we all descend on you.

To Tony Stericker, thanks Dad for the Cornish memories and to you and Mel for supporting me in some of my theatrical endeavours. I hope you will come out here soon.

To our second family, my lovely aunt and uncle Caroline and Nigel Webb, your love and support for us Stericker girls has been a constant in our lives for which we are most grateful. And love to cousins Amanda Tiddy and Nic Webb and your families; Nigel, Rob, Izzy, Cameron and Maya. Come back and visit soon.

Thanks for all the games and fun from our gorgeous nieces and nephews: Lola and Otto Chambers, Harvey and Theo Steventon and Saoirse, Johnjo and Aiobhe Murphy. Thank you Maria O'Neill for being a great sister-in-law and to Conor Murphy for being such a talented musician, always agreeing to play at the family weddings and funerals. Love to Helen O'Neill and Gerry Kelly for the cards and the scrabble.

Thank you Sarah and Jim Dalton, Megan, Matt and Dan for the wonderful Scillies memories that were such an important part of Daisy and Holly's childhood. And to James and Peggie Terry and Becca Clark for that incredible Canada trip. We are looking forward to your visit to us here very soon.

Thank you Tec Beint for the extraordinarily memorable festival and musical experiences for me and the girls.

Thank you to our old friends for all your support in our move, for visiting us several times here in Quillan and keeping us in touch with our old lives: Brigette Martin and Tec Beint, Deb and Rich Bunn, Sarah and Jim Dalton, Parissa, Chris and Arianna Card, Gynna and David Holmes, Garrath and Michelle Ellershaw, Buffy and Graeme Harrison, Phil Rees and Anne Owen and Bridget McMullan. Thank you Ben Dunn for publishing advice and trusting me with your fabulous books. Thank you to Kate Ellis and Greg Coomber and Elmarie and Léan Marnewick for all the support and love you gave us in Africa. And to Jess and Pete Gilgan for helping us through those initial tough baby years. We hope you'll visit soon.

Many thanks for the friendship and love of our new friends here in Quillan. There are so many good people here who give generously of their time to help others, too many to name everyone. But special mention to my fellow writers and their partners — our friends Nick Plumbridge, Jim Towle, Earl Rinehart, Bryan Wetherill, Clive Davies, Gareth Nolan, Liam O'Neill and Tassilo Kubitz. Thank you also to Derrick Campbell and Kris Smith who are such an important part of our community. Love to Steph and Matt Holister, Tess King and Mark Shepherd who come and go. Can't wait for our next camper van adventure.

We are blessed to have wonderful neighbours here who have become good friends, cook delicious meals for us and are happy to feed our cat Brutus. Thank you Bruno Santini and Gary Rowe; Peter Clifford and Tricia Dair.

Finally, heartfelt thanks to my best friend and love Matthew O'Neill for your laughter and fun and encouragement of my crazy ideas, for putting up with me and feeding me for the last thirty-four years. May we have many more adventures together my darling.

Printed in Great Britain
by Amazon

44457354R00089